AF366118

1939-1945
WORLD WAR TWO

AUTORI

Paolo Crippa, Paolo Crippa, (23 April 1978) has been cultivating a passion for Italian history, especially World War II, since high school. His research focuses mainly on the field of military history and in particular on armoured units from the 1930s until the end of the Second World War. In 2006, he published his first volume, "I Reparti Corazzati della Repubblica Sociale Italiana 1943/1945", the first organic research completed and published in Italy on the subject, followed by "Duecento Volti della R.S.I." (2007), "Un anno con il 27° Reggimento Artiglieria Legnano" (2011) and "I reparti controguerriglia della R.S.I." (2020). (2020). He has more than forty articles to his credit for the journals Milites, Historica Nuova, SGM - Second World War, Batailes & Blindes, Ritterkreuz, Fronti di Guerra, Mezzi Corazzati, Storia & Battaglie, Umago Viva, La Martinella and Storia del Novecento, both as an author and in collaboration with other researchers and has carried out collaborations and consultancies for other authors in the drafting of historical - uniformological texts. Since 2019 he has collaborated with Luca Cristini Editore in the realisation of the series "Witness to War" and since 2020 he has been its Director. With Mattioli 1885 he published "Italia 43-45. The armoured vehicles of civil war" (2014), "I mezzi corazzati italiani della guerra civile 1943-1945" (2015) and "Italia 43-45. The vehicles of the cobelligerent units" (2018).

Antonio Tallillo was born on 3 March 1958 and lives and works in Verona. 'Thunderstruck' by modelling since his school days (circa 1972), since 1977 he has found his true vocation in historical-modelling popularisation, in a close commonality of ideas with his brother Andrea, who has remained a 'pure' modeller. His main historical interests concern military vehicles, especially armoured ones, used in the First and Second World War (1916-1945). More recently, the focus has been on those of our Army, and in the field of uniformology, they concern the two world wars. Alone, or more often in collaboration with his brother Andrea, he has published countless historical and modelling articles in national magazines and in the newsletters of various associations, as well as for six Internet sites. Since the early 2000s, he has co-authored seven books published with GMT, two for Edizioni Ardite, and has collaborated with iconographic material and texts for another 14 books by various publishers.

PUBLISHING'S NOTES

LICENSES COMMONS

Title: **ITALIAN ARMOURED VEHICLES IN RUSSIA 1941-1944** Code.: **WTW-039 EN** By Paolo Crippa and Antonio Tallillo

ISBN code: 978-88-93279178 First edition December 2022

Text: English Nr. of images: 127 dimensione: 177,8x254mm Cover & Art Design: Luca S. Cristini

WITNESS TO WAR (SOLDIERSHOP) is a trademark of Luca Cristini Editore, via Orio, 35/4 - 24050 Zanica (BG) ITALY.

WITNESS TO WAR

ITALIAN ARMOURED VEHICLES IN RUSSIA 1941 - 1944

PHOTOS & IMAGES FROM WORLD WARTIME ARCHIVES

PAOLO CRIPPA – ANTONIO TALLILLO

BOOKS TO COLLECT

CONTENTS

ITALIAN ARMOURED VEHICLES IN RUSSIA

The disastrous Russian Campaign conducted by the *Regio Esercito* saw a marginal participation of Italian armoured units, which achieved poor results. In fact, only three armoured units were sent to the Soviet Union, equipped, moreover, with tanks and light self-propelled vehicles, which could only compete with other light armoured units or infantry and not against the Soviet heavy tanks, and in an absolutely inadequate number for the scale of the conflict that was taking place on that front. There were two Cavalry units (the III Gruppo Gruppo Squadroni Corazzato *"San Giorgio"* on L3 tanks and the XIII Gruppo Squadroni Semoventi *"Cavalleggeri di Alessandria"* on L40 tanks) and one of Bersaglieri (Il LXVII Battaglione Bersaglieri Motocorazzato on L6/40 tanks), all of which were attached, at different times, to the *'Principe Amedeo Duca d'Aosta'* Celere Division.

They were flanked by a paltry Autoblinde Platoon of the *'Nizza Cavalry'* Regiment, equipped with only two AB41 armoured cars, part of the *'Vicenza'* Division, which could do no other thing apart providing support in reconnaissance actions.

An attempt to reinforce the armoured units in the Soviet Union was made on 6 October 1942, when 24 90/53 self-propelled vehicles of the 10th Regiment and the DLVII Self-Propelled 75/18 Group were allocated to the 8th Army (A.R.M.I.R.), but, for undecipherable reasons, these units were never sent to Russia: this was a serious mistake, only sending more powerful armoured vehicles could have had any influence on operations on the Eastern Front.

Their contribution to the operations was also limited, but it can be rightly assumed that they deserved the respect that any Italian fighter who used the same few and outdated armoured vehicles deserves, amidst a thousand difficulties, always facing an adversary rich in equipment and machines, supported from the air in an overwhelming manner.

After the Armistice, a group of former Arditi fought on Russian soil on board AS42 trucks, in support of the German 2nd Parachute Division, being appreciated for their courage and determination, even in the difficult situation of the German troops on the Eastern Front.

'Principe Amedeo Duca d'Aosta' Celere Division (P.A.D.A.)

Descendant of the 3rd Lombardy Cavalry Division, the *'Principe Amedeo Duca d'Aosta'* Celere Division (P.A.D.A.) was formed in Milan on 1 November 1934, incorporating the 3rd Celere Brigade 'P.A.D.A.' and the 3rd Celere Artillery Regiment (Articelere) 'P.A.D.A.'. With Italy's entry into the war in 1940, the division was moved from Cividale del Friuli to the Borgo San Dalmazzo - Cuneo area, as an Army Reserve within the framework of the Battle of the Western Alps, without seeing operational deployment. Sent to the Italian-Yugoslav border, on 13 April 1941 it entered enemy territory, reaching Jelenje, Kubjak, Cakovac and Slunj in the following days. On the 20th, the units occupied Rakovica, Drazik Grad, Bihac and on the 22nd, Trogir, Split and Karlovac. In Split, the Division was engaged in combing operations until 31 May.

In July 1941, after incorporating the 107th 47/32 Anti-tank Company, the Division was incorporated into the Italian Expeditionary Corps in Russia (C.S.I.R.) and transferred to the Botoşani area on the Vltava: under its command there was the only armoured unit of the Corps, the III Armoured Squadron Group *"San Giorgio"*. The Division's units followed the front line, which was moving rapidly eastwards, deploying in September at Dniprod-zeržyns'k on the Dnepr, on the right of the 9th Infantry Division *"Pasubio"*, engaging in re-connaissance patrol actions, hand-to-hand combat and artillery clashes. On 28 September, it crossed the Dnjepr targeting Warwarowka, Jelissawtowka and then Petrikowka, comple-ting the encirclement manoeuvre conducted from the north by the *"Pasubio"* Division and from the south-east by the 52nd *"Torino"* Infantry Division.

In early November, with an enveloping manoeuvre, it occupied the industrial and mining centre of Rikowo and, in the following days, Gorlowka and Nikitowka. The advance of the Axis troops was then blocked by Soviet resistance and the so-called 'Christmas counter-of-fensive' on 25 December 1941.

In January 1942, the Division repelled continuous Soviet attacks, which were everywhere contained and repulsed. In February it assisted in operations to contain enemy units wed-ged in the German-held lines at Izyum and, from 17 to 31 May, it supported the counter-at-tack to break through the Izyum creek.

At the same time, in the first half of 1942, the Division underwent a radical transformation, giving up some units (at the end of February, the *'San Giorgio'* was withdrawn from the front line and, in July, was sent to Italy) and receiving, among others, the Croatian Legion, a foreign unit of the Royal Army. In addition, in July, the 13th L40 Self-propelled Group of the 14th *"Cavalry of Alexandria"* Regiment and the LXVII Bersaglieri Motorised Battalion arrived; with these units and the 3rd Bersaglieri Regiment already in force, the large unit assumed the order of a Motorised Division.

Placed under the 6th German Army, it reached Voroschilovgrad on 25 July, crossing the Donetz the next day and establishing itself on the Millerowo line. After a period of rearran-gement in the rear, on 20 August, during the first Russian offensive on the Don, the Division supported the 2nd Infantry Division *"Sforzesca"*, blocking the enemy advance on the right bank of the great river. After a long period of relative calm, on 22 December, the bulk of the P.A.D.A. began to retreat with the "Southern Block" towards Dnjepropetrovsk, Polta-va, Krassnojarovka and Jessa Ulof, while some of its divisions belonging to the "Northern Block", barricaded in the Tcertkovo stronghold, were targeted by Soviet attacks.

The unit, by then decimated and in constant difficulty due to the fall back, finally reached Donez in early 1943 and returned to the homeland in April, where it was gradually recon-stituted according to its original physiognomy as a Celere Division, but was disbanded on 15 September 1943, following the armistice events.

The Celere Division, far from the expected exploits, turned out to be hybrid, difficult to de-ploy in a compact manner and with well amalgamated units, ending up being dismembered and used to provide support to other units.

▲ On long transports, the men and vehicles of the Regio Esercito reached the icy Russian lands, where they were involved in one of the most senseless campaigns of the Second World War. Pictured are FIAT 626 trucks of the 'Vicenza' Division.

▲ Italian truck in trouble due to mud: 'General Winter', who had already helped the Russians at the time of the Napoleonic invasion, proved to be a formidable ally against the Italian-German troops as well.

▼ During the Russian Campaign, logistics were of paramount importance and the effort required of the Autieri units was considerable. In this picture, a column of trucks of the 34th Heavy Autocentre marching on Russian soil: the second truck performs the anti-aircraft protection of the vehicles, being armed with a machine gun in the body, while all the other trucks have camouflage masking on the tarpaulin.

III ARMOURED SQUADRON GROUP 'SAN GIORGIO'

From the end of October 1933, the 19th Regiment *Cavalleggeri Guide* of Parma became a mechanised unit, one of its Squadron Groups was transformed into a *Gruppo Squadroni Carri Veloci*, acting as a training and testing centre. From January to June 1934, 3 Groups were created, initially with 3 Squadrons of 13 tanks each:

- I Group *'San Marco'*
- The *'San Giusto'* Group
- Group III *'San Martino'*.

By the end of November 1934, it had also been decided to include a CV 33 Tank Squadron (the 5th Squadron out of 15 vehicles) in the staff of each Cavalry Regiment, starting with the 1st *'Nizza'*, 14th *'Alessandria'* and 6th *'Aosta'*, but by October 1938, these Squadrons, only 6 in all, were disbanded and only the three completed units from the spring of 1935 for the Celeri Divisions and a few minor units remained 'Cavalry'.

When the Italian Expeditionary Forces in Russia (C.S.I.R.) departed for the vast Russian territories on 10 July 1941, the only tank unit mobilised for the front was the III Gruppo Squadroni Armorati *'San Giorgio'*, part of the 3rd Celere Division *'Principe Amedeo d'Aosta'* (also known by its acronym 'PADA'); organised into four squadrons, the group was equipped exclusively with 53 L3 light tanks of the 33, 35 and 38 versions. The Group had recently returned to Italy, to its barracks in Verona, after having participated, albeit for a short period, in the Yugoslavian Campaign and was organised on:

- Command Squadron *"San Giorgio"*[1]
- 1st *"Delle Armi"* Squadron
- 2nd *"Medaglie d'Oro"* Squadron
- 3rd *"Savoy"* Squadron
- 4th *"Novara"* Squadron

The units reached Borsa in Hungary by train, after a 25-day journey, and from there they moved on to Botosani in Romanian Moldavia by their own means, a journey of around 200 km.

At the beginning of August, the tanks of the *"San Giorgio"* Group took part in the so-called "Battle of the Two Rivers" (10 August - 26 September 1941), a major manoeuvre carried out by the German armed forces to trap the Soviets between the Dniestr and Bug rivers. The *'Pasubio'* Division took part in the battle, which was the first clash for Italian troops on Russian soil; the *'San Giorgio'* Group supported a breakthrough action near Jwanovya on 23 September together with a German Kampfgruppe, while, after losing its first five tanks in a clash at Saderokowka, it helped repel a Soviet counter-attack attempt at Tsaritschanka on the 26th.

---

1 Under the command of Major Evasio Malinverni, the Squadron consisted of nine tanks with the following names: St George, Geniere, Seaman, General Marié, General Mariotti, S. Foca, Natisone Valley, Pradis, Selz.

The "San Giorgio" Group was also attached to the "Pasubio" Division during the operations at Petrikowka between 28 and 30 September, which took place on a front of over 50 km, during the battle of Stalino (which also aimed to control the mining centres of Gorlowka and Rykowo and the Trudewaya station, where the great Caspian Sea pipeline ran) and the battle of Nikitowka. Here, the Group lost several tanks during the Soviet siege that lasted from 6 to 12 November, which held a section of the Division's 80th Regiment.

With only forty or so surviving tanks and after penetrating almost 1,400 km into enemy territory, the 'San Giorgio' also took part in the infamous 'Battle of Christmas'. The C.S.I.R. divisions were hit by a powerful attack led by two Cavalry divisions (the 35th and 68th) and strong enemy Infantry divisions (74th, 136th, 265th and 296th Infantry Divisions); the Italian troops managed to contain the enemy impact, at the cost of very heavy losses.

The harsh winter weather contributed to putting the last surviving tanks out of action, and the soldiers of the "San Giorgio" Group, now dismounted, were merged into the "Musinu" Regiment, made up of a "Lancieri di Montebello" Group, a Motorized Artillery Battery of the 8th Artillery Regiment, a Battalion of Bersaglieri and two Battalions of Pontieri. The Regiment was a formation unit, amounting to a little over 1,300 men, and fought in the Izyum salient, with the German 17.Armee, following the breakthrough of the front by the Soviets (late January - late February 1942), with the very few surviving tanks practically unusable due to lack of spare parts.

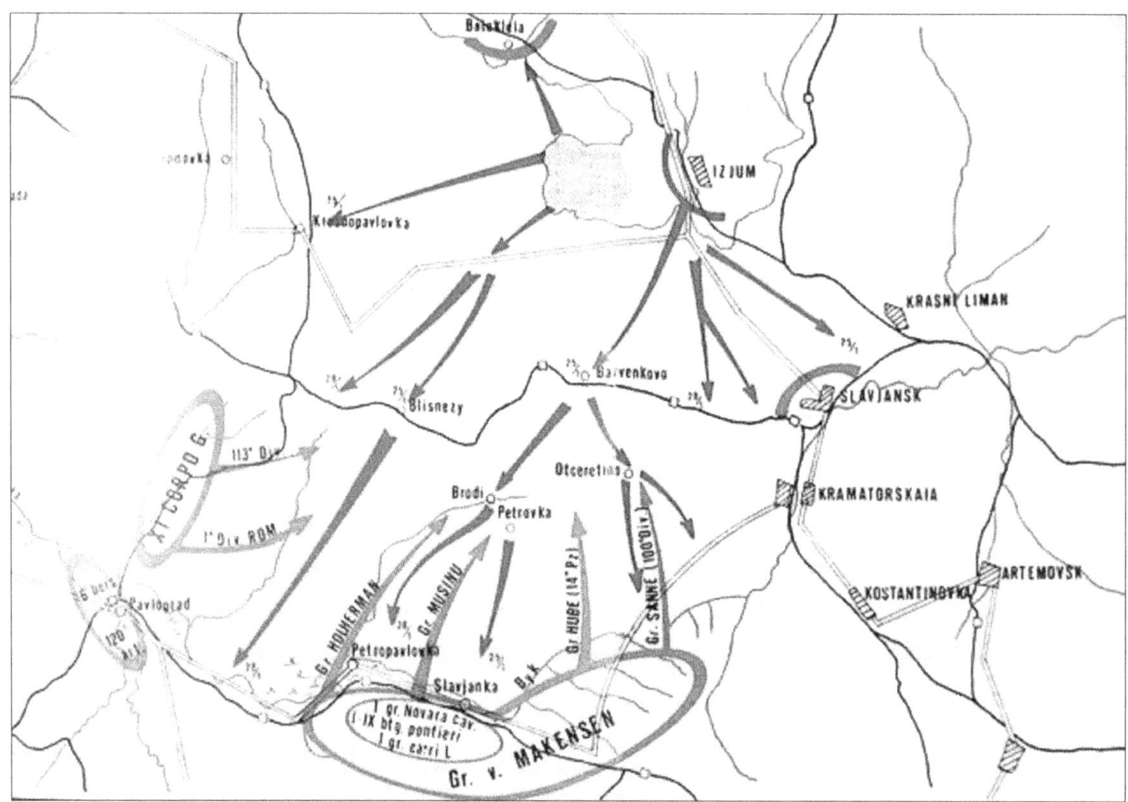

▲ Map of the fighting that took place between the end of January and the end of February 1942 in the Izyum salient, where Soviet units operated from the north to break through the front held by the German 17.Armee. Along with it also fought the "Musinu" Regiment (bottom centre on the map), of which the "San Giorgio" Armoured Squadron Group, now practically without tanks and dismounted, was part.

At the end of February, the *San Giorgio* was withdrawn from the front line and was placed in a defensive position in anticipation of the fine weather, but, as it now had no offensive potential and could not be re-equipped, it began to return home on 15 July 1942.

Collective decoration granted to military personnel of the department

Bronze Medal for Military Valour
At the end of the Russian Campaign, for its commitment during ten months in hostile territory, the pennant of the *"San Giorgio"* Group was decorated with the Bronze Medal for Military Valour, with the following motivation: *"With sure boldness marked by the noble traditions of the Force from which he is descended, fighting alongside the rapid units and in competition with the infantry, during ten months of a very hard campaign, he demonstrated frank courage and generous impetus, both when with his agile tanks he had to open the way to the vanguards, and when in the alternating and culminating hours of the defensive battle, the prohibitive conditions of the winter season and the imperative demands of the fight forced him to go on foot. Russian Front, August 1941 - May 1942"*.

Individual decorations awarded to military personnel of the department

Silver Medals for Military Valour
- Barillari Gaspare, cavalryman of the 3rd Tank Squadron Group L *San Giorgio*;
- Bottoni Gibel, second lieutenant in the 3rd Tank Squadron Group L *San Giorgio* (*in memory*);
- Buffoli Angelo, corporal of the 3rd Tank Squadron Group L *San Giorgio* (*in memory*);
- Ceccarelli Arivio, Staff Sergeant of the 3rd Tank Squadron Group L *San Giorgio*;
- Corradini Alceo, complementary lieutenant in the 3rd Tank Squadron Group L *San Giorgio* (*in memory*);
- Lovati Luigi, lieutenant of III Tank Squadron Group L *San Giorgio*;
- Martini Gaetano, cavalryman of the 3rd Tank Squadron Group L *San Giorgio*;
- Miglio Mario, cavalryman of the 3rd Tank Squadron Group L *San Giorgio*;
- Nicolini Fernando, lieutenant of the 3rd Tank Squadron Group L *San Giorgio*.
- Ramella Carlo, corporal of III Tank Squadron Group L *San Giorgio*;
- Rampin Antonio, complementary lieutenant of III Tank Squadron Group L *San Giorgio*.

Bronze Medal for Military Valour

- Alfieri Cesare, sergeant of the 3rd Tank Squadron Group L 'San Giorgio';
- Colombo Pietro, cavalryman of the 3rd Tank Squadron Group L 'San Giorgio' (*in memory*);
- Cutolo Giovanni, captain in s.p.e. of III Tank Squadron Group L 'San Giorgio';
- Lenotti Alessandro, second lieutenant in the 3rd Tank Squadron Group L 'San Giorgio';
- Lucania Pietro, Sergeant Major, 3rd Tank Squadron Group L 'San Giorgio';
- Marinelli Roano, knight of the 3rd group (squadron) L 'San Giorgio' tanks, 2nd Squadron (*in memory*).
- Maruzzo Ottavio, Staff Sergeant of the 3rd Tank Squadron Group L 'San Giorgio';
- Meneghello Guerrino, corporal of III Tank Squadron Group L 'San Giorgio';
- Moretti Cristoforo, corporal of III Tank Squadron Group L 'San Giorgio' (*in memory*);
- Perricone Michele, corporal, 3rd Tank Squadron Group L 'San Giorgio';
- Piccinini Amedeo, sergeant of the 3rd Tank Squadron Group L 'San Giorgio';
- Rocca Gino, corporal of III Tank Squadron Group L 'San Giorgio';
- Rota Guido, corporal of III Tank Squadron Group L 'San Giorgio';
- Scavino Guido, Lance Corporal, 3rd Tank Squadron Group L 'San Giorgio' (*in memory*);
- Teodori Dante, second lieutenant in the 3rd Tank Squadron Group L 'San Giorgio';
- Vento Giovanni, captain in s.p.e. of III Tank Squadron Group L 'San Giorgio'.

Military Cross for Valour

- Arrigo Mario, knight of the III Group L tank squadron 'San Giorgio' (*in memory*);
- Carbonini Carlo, cavalryman of III Tank Squadron Group L 'San Giorgio';
- Cianci Angelo, second lieutenant in the 3rd Tank Squadron Group L 'San Giorgio';
- Filippini Angelo, knight of the 3rd Tank Squadron Group L 'San Giorgio' (*in memory*);
- Gaggini Pietro, cavalryman of the 3rd Tank Squadron Group L 'San Giorgio' (*in memory*);
- Gorlato Antonio, corporal of III Tank Squadron Group L 'San Giorgio';
- Lovisetto Pietro, sergeant of III Tank Squadron Group L 'San Giorgio';
- Massarotto Guerrino, cavalryman of the 3rd Tank Squadron Group L 'San Giorgio';

- Moscato Francesco, corporal of III Tank Squadron Group L 'San Giorgio';
- Sarfatti Gustavo, complementary lieutenant in the 3rd Tank Squadron Group L 'San Giorgio';
- Slanzi Carlo, cavalryman of III Tank Squadron Group L 'San Giorgio';
- Tomei Renato, sergeant of III Tank Squadron Group L 'San Giorgio' (in memory);
- Turina Lino, cavalryman of the 3rd Tank Squadron Group L 'San Giorgio'.

▲ A self-propelled 47/32 L40: some examples were used in Russia by the Alexandria Cavalry.

▲ Tanks of the *'San Giorgio'* Armoured Squadron Group pass through a small town in Romania on their way to the Russian front (Benvenuti - Colonna).

▲ The tanks of the *'San Giorgio'* Armoured Squadron Group in Russia.

▲ A L3/38 light tank of the *'San Giorgio'* among a group of Russian isbas (Benvenuti - Colonna).

▼ A FIAT 626 truck of the 34th Heavyweight Autocentre advances circumspectly over an unstable wooden bridge, which crosses a Russian watercourse.

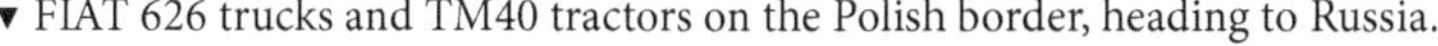

▲ L3 tanks engaged in crossing the Dniepr River on a bridge thrown by German engineers (Benvenuti - Colonna).

▼ FIAT 626 trucks and TM40 tractors on the Polish border, heading to Russia.

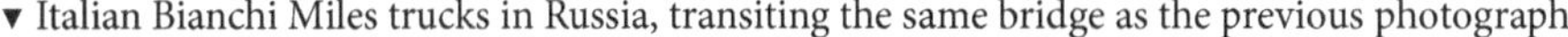

▲ In the course of operations against the Soviets, heavy trucks were also used, such as this FIAT 666, which was engaged in crossing a bridge built by the Genio del Regio Esercito.

▼ Italian Bianchi Miles trucks in Russia, transiting the same bridge as the previous photograph.

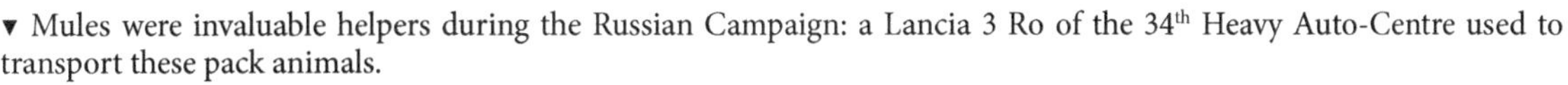

▲ L3/33 of the *'San Giorgio'* on the march during the November 1941 operations in the Donetz Basin (Benvenuti - Colonna).

▼ Mules were invaluable helpers during the Russian Campaign: a Lancia 3 Ro of the 34th Heavy Auto-Centre used to transport these pack animals.

▲ Tanks of the *'San Giorgio'* Group on the move in the rear of the front in the autumn of 1941 (Benvenuti - Colonna).

▼ Transfer to the front of a platoon of CV35s, in the middle of a car column returning from it.

▲ A rare military bus on a Bianchi Miles chassis in Russia.

▼ A soldier from the *'San Giorgio'* Squadron Group in the freezing Russian winter: at that time, the *'San Giorgio'* was part of the *'Musinu'* (Vaccari) Tactical Group.

▲ Second Lieutenant Gibel Bottoni was awarded the Silver Medal of Military Valour for his behaviour during the battle that involved Sofiewka, Petrowka and Klinowj between 16 and 25 February 1942. The second lieutenant was born in Bologna on 15 December 1916 and was enrolled in the third year of the Faculty of Economics at the outbreak of war. Enlisted (or perhaps he left voluntarily for the war, it is not clear) he was assigned with the rank of second lieutenant to the Command Squadron of the 3rd Tank Group L3 *'San Giorgio'*. On 5 November 1942, the University of Bologna awarded him the Laurea Honoris Causa alla memoria. His mortal remains were repatriated on 19 September 1992 and reassembled in the Temple of Cargnacco (UD).

▲ The Silver Medal for Military Valour for Second Lieutenant Gibel Bottoni, who fell between 17 and 18 February 1942. This is the motivation: *"Commander of a platoon defending an important advanced position, for two days he tenaciously resisted the repeated attacks of preponderant forces and several times he launched himself, at the head of the employees, to counterattack, succeeding in driving back the enemy after inflicting considerable losses. In the course of a new and more violent adversary attack, with the resolute will to maintain the position entrusted to him, as a last desperate attempt he hurled himself at the head of the survivors, on the overpowering enemy and turned him once again to flight, in this action he fell valiantly. Ssofiewka (Russian front), 17-18 February 1942"*.

▲ A sergeant of the III Armoured Squadron Group *'San Giorgio'* next to his L3/35 tank in Russia (Tallillo).

LXVII MOTORISED BERSAGLIERI BATTALION

At the same time as the withdrawal of the *'San Giorgio'* Armoured Squadron Group, the LXVII Bersaglieri Motorised Battalion arrived in Russia from Italy, equipped with 58 L6/40 light tanks, which was destined for the Eastern Front, despite the limitations demonstrated by this tank, due to the lack of other means. Formed in Siena a few months earlier (officially on 25 February) with the means of the 2nd and 3rd Companies of the LXVIII Twin Battalion (in training) and personnel taken from the 5th and 18th Bersaglieri Regiments, the mobilisation phase was laborious for the unit, involving a training cycle in San Quirino (PN), with temporary assignment to the 'Centauro' Armoured Division. However, the need had arisen to replace the L3 tanks of the *'San Giorgio'* Group on the Eastern Front and so the unit, through a long rail journey, arrived on the Eastern Front on 12 July 1942, under the command of Major Bartolucci. The Battalion was assigned, like the 3rd Group L Tank Squadron *'San Giorgio'*, to the 3rd Celere Division 'PADA' (Principe Amedeo Duca D'Aosta) and was organised on:

- Command Platoon
- 1st Company on 5 Platoons with 5 tanks each
- 2nd Company on 5 Platoons with 5 tanks each[2]

for a total of 58 vehicles. Some of them were of the Radio version, assigned to the Command Platoon in pairs. These were standard tanks equipped with a second two-way radio (RF 2 CA) in addition to the standard RF 1 CA. The radio had a range of 20 km in telegraphy and 15 km in voice when the tank was stationary, but in order to fit it, part of the on-board 20 mm ammunition was sacrificed. The range was, however, insufficient under actual conditions of use and required frequent valve changes. Externally, the version was recognisable by the second antenna, located at the rear of the superstructure.

The unusual presence of a fifth tank Platoon can be explained by the fact that, as the front line was very far from Italy and therefore from the wards' depots, sending tanks to replace losses was very difficult and this fifth Platoon would therefore fulfil the role of a reserve, from which replacement armoured vehicles could be drawn. For long-range transfers, the small frontal footprint of the vehicles also allowed them to be transported on the platform of medium-sized trucks such as the FIAT 666.

By mid-August, the Battalion was in the area of Novo Gorlowka, after an almost 100-kilometre journey by track to Donetz. From Novo Gorlowka the unit departed at dawn on 25 August, arriving in the early afternoon hours in Tarassovka. The unit, together with the 5th Alpine Regiment, was destined to attack the ridge of Quota 222.4 (Jagodnj). At around 09:00, Lieutenant Albanese's 2nd Company was ordered to move to a nearby location and prepare to carry out a counter-attack, while Captain Ottaviani's 1st Company continued to fine-tune their equipment.

---

2 Respectively the former 2nd Company and the former 3rd Company of the 18th Bersaglieri Regiment.

In the afternoon, some officers carried out a reconnaissance on foot, pushing beyond the Italian line. The order was for the Tank Company, in two groups and by two different routes, to reach that altitude, followed by a Battalion of the 5th Alpine on that rough terrain, but without difficulty for the tanks. But night passed and the order was not confirmed.

On 27 August, the unit sustained its first combat in Russia: two Platoons with 12 tanks contributed to the defensive manoeuvre carried out by the *'Valchiese'* and *'Vestone'* Battalions of the 3rd Alpine Regiment, repelling a Russian attack in the Jagodnj sector. The results were discreet, although four tanks were lost and the same number seriously damaged.

Meanwhile, the 2nd Company was deployed on 1 September in the Bolskoj sector in support of the *"Valchiese"* Alpine Battalion, with an attack that ended with the occupation of Quarters 236.7 and 209. Three platoons had been sent out from different points, with the task of occupying the heights in front, which divided our Don line into a precise area. But while the central platoon had reached its objective, beating enemy resistance and destroying an anti-tank battery, the other two platoons on the sides had been blocked by enemy units. At that juncture, the Alpine troops, given their deployment characteristics, could not be of much help, in an action whose outcome was determined solely by mobility and firepower. The opposing units, although initially surprised, had reoccupied the heights with concentric attacks. The losses for the Bersaglieri tank men were 3 tanks lost, 4 men killed and 3 wounded. The most seriously wounded was a tank leader officer, who was brought back immediately and, thanks to a German plane that had landed expressly in the area, was taken to the Voroshilovgrad hospital shortly afterwards.

The following is an excerpt from the report of 6 September 1942 by Lieutenant Albanese, commander of the 2nd Tank Company of the LXVII Battalion, concerning this unfortunate battle:

"On 31 August 1942, the 2nd Tank Company was ordered to split into two platoons and Company Headquarters and make itself available to the "Vestone" Battalion (6th Alpini) for an offensive action to be carried out on Quota 236.2 and 209.6, west of Bolschoj. The attack of the three Companies of the "Vestone" began at 3 p.m. on 1 September, after a very brief artillery preparation, with departure on Quota 228. The 1st tank platoon had the task of overtaking the left company and eliminating any resistance along the direction of the attack, as well as heading for Quota 236.2. After a few minutes, the platoon reached a blockhouse called "Ferma 4", where it stopped to reorganise, proceeding immediately afterwards to Quota 236.8. The vanguard tank platoon lost a tank but continued, near the objective an enemy artillery battery was uncovered and eliminated, but then a strong Russian counter-attack started and forced an Alpine company to retreat to its starting position. The 2nd platoon was sent to Quota 209.6 to cooperate with an Alpine company that had failed to continue. Once past the "Ferma 4" blockhouse, the platoon suffered a strong anti-tank reaction and the loss of 3 tanks and damage to another. The surviving tanks continued, but when they arrived near the objective, seeing the left Alpine Company retreating and the right Alpine Company unable to get through, they fell back to their starting position. The losses amounted to 8 tanks in all, as well as 8 tankers. When the action was over, 3 tanks and volunteer crews returned to the contested area and managed to recover an immobilised tank".

Apparently, there were no other notable battles afterwards, and least of all against enemy armour.

From 2 to 8 September, the Company was moved to Obelitze, then to the area northwest of Rubaskin and finally, in part, with the command of the 1st Company and two tank platoons, to the area south of Quota 208.4, as a reserve. After the end of the month, Romanian troops came to relieve LXVII Battalion and as they were handed over, LXVII assembled about 20 kilometres west in the area of Werchmashai, with 2nd Company about ten kilometres west of Werchrusili. After twenty days or so, it was taken over by Romanian troops and was assigned in early November to the area around Sagrebalovka, some thirty kilometres west of Bogucar, reuniting with several other units of the Celere Division. The move was very strenuous, especially due to a sudden and vertiginous drop in temperatures and the first snow. With the thermometer at -20°C, it took a lot of effort to get the L6 engines moving again, the only positive note being the distribution of excellent winter clothing in large numbers. In November, the unit was withdrawn from the line to reorganise as far as possible. It was able to take part in a battle around the 20th in the Meskov ona, in support of the German 318th Infantry Regiment, where the tank leaders were unable to use their rifle scopes, which were always fogged up, nor their periscopes, nor could they turn their turrets because the grease on their rolling crowns had frozen, and had to rely fully on their pilots, who at least had a hyposcope at their disposal, to roughly aim at the enemy units and hit them.

On 11 December 1942, together with the self-propelled tanks on the same hull of the XIII Cavalry Group Alexandria, the L6s of the Battalion returned to combat, in the centre of the very long sector held by the A. R. M. I. R. , in a section that had remained uncovered, in support of the Italian Infantry Divisions 'Cosseria' and *Ravenna* and some German divisions, which were already under pressure. The effective tanks were very few, less than twenty, due to the lack of supplies and spare parts, and supported only by 22 German guns. After the battle of Dubowkoff on 16 December, the 1st Company with its 13 tanks was ordered to retreat to Krasni and to report to the Infantry Division "Cosseria". It arrived there without 4 tanks, which were stopped due to serious breakdowns. At noon on 18 December, with only 8 tanks, it headed towards Saki. At 550 metres south of that village, it organised a line of resistance, with the tanks arranged at intervals of 150 - 200 metres from each other and with the help of engineer squads, 4 Breda 37 machine guns and 2 20 mm machine guns on the left; the command was taken by Major Irandi of the "Cosseria". After two hours of night fighting, the sappers' squads, lacking ammunition, fell back into the village, which was subjected to an aerial bombardment at around 2 a.m. and was evacuated by the German defenders. The tanks, with ammunition at a minimum, fell back to Iwanowka after the loss of 3 damaged and 3 wounded and 11 second-degree frozen among their crews. The retreat to Krasni, although it was only 15 kilometres away, took place under terrible conditions and very slowly, due to the deep snow and the impossibility of starting the five tanks available, apart from a couple that were used to pull the others. The supplied cables proved to be weak, and one had to make do 'Italian style' by literally tying them in knots at the worst. The tanks fortunately joined up with a truck of the *Cosseria* Division that was doing the same route.

After an hour, a stationary column of troops was reached, in which five more L6 tanks from another platoon were found. Arriving in Krasni, the Company was first ordered to deploy to defend the front north of the town, then after a few hours it was ordered to abandon it, first destroying the Subsistence stores. The crews took advantage of this to 'save' cigarettes, tuna cans, tins of sardines and meat, blankets and shoes, piling everything in and on top of the vehicles, before blowing everything up. After several stages of a terrible night march, they arrived at 10:30 a.m. on 18 December in Kantemirowka, with only two tanks, used to transport the wounded and frozen. At dawn on the 19th, Kantemirowka was swarming with troops, alerted by the arrival over a hill above of two Soviet T-3 tanks, which began shelling the station buildings. At this juncture, Bersaglier and other specialised troops took on the heavy burden of covering the retreat of other units, but the dreadful weather conditions and confusion between commands did not allow for any really effective action.

Meanwhile, on 16 December, the 2nd Company, reduced to one platoon, and the Battalion Headquarters were in Gadjutscheye and could not cope with an attack preceded by Soviet tanks at 6 a.m. the next day, falling back towards Kanetemirowka, where in the early hours of the 18th they were hit by another armoured attack. In Gadjutscheye, the march sergeant Giorgio Dell'Amico distinguished himself, who, after trying to repair his tank marked "RE 4050", had to sabotage it, but nevertheless opened the way between an incoming enemy patrol and took enemy prisoners, receiving a solemn Army Corps Citation from the commander of the II Corps, General Zanghieri[3]. At 8 a.m. on 19 December, the columned tanks were caught under fire from the enemy tanks and, without orders, moved towards Bedowok, still being tailed by Soviet tanks. The L6s were able to stop for a few hours in Bedowok for vehicle maintenance: the last known incident was the defence of the 'Rex' bridge over the Donetz at Wessalajagora, with the last efficient armoured tanks. Many of the surviving L6 tanks were destroyed in the fighting at Filonovo, in a desperate attempt to cover the most endangered sectors of the *"Ravenna"* Division, but the adversary was superior in every respect. The very few surviving vehicles joined a retreating column, which reached the rear lines on 28 December at Skassirkaja, but no L6/40s from the Battalion managed to return home. The unit left for Italy on 22 March 1943, stationed at the Siena Depot and was disbanded on 8 July of the same year.

---

3 *"II Corps Headquarters*
Solemn Citation of C.A.
- availing myself of the power conferred on me by Rule 536 of the R.E. Disciplinary Rules. I hereby award a solemn C.A. citation (to be inscribed)
to Sergeant Dell'Amico Giorgio di Michele
belonging to the LXVIIth armoured bersaglieri btg.
on the following grounds:
"Radio petty officer, in the presence of an incursion of enemy tanks, which had already bypassed the position, seeing the stationary tank in avarice, remained in place to restore it to efficiency.
Threatened by the enemy's increasing offensives he continued in the risky task until, having made recovery impossible even with the trailer, he destroyed the tank's organs and evaded capture by breaking through enemy scouting elements, capturing prisoners. An example of tenacious will and disregard for danger'.
Gadjutscheye (Russia) on 17 December 1942/XXI
Zone of operations there 15 January 1943/XXI
The C.A. Commanding General
G. Zanghieri'.

It is, of course, difficult to make a calm judgement on the L6/40's use on the Eastern Front; it certainly did not make an effective contribution, even though it was more or less comparable to the Panzer II at the time of its adoption. Despite the fact that the Bersaglieri's L6 appeared in more than one newsreel and photo report, as if it were modern material available in large numbers, the tank revealed all its weaknesses during the months spent on the Eastern Front. Small, but with a silhouette that was too visible even from a distance, it was inferior to enemy vehicles of the same class in protection and mobility, so much so that during the clashes at Gorbatowo even the tall grass, jamming into the suspension, reduced the speed of the tanks to 15 km/h, and the armoured vehicle was therefore unsuitable for exploration. In addition, the unit's command, before leaving for the eastern front, had already reported that the trailing cables were excessively weak, but to no avail.

Both for transport and for recovery in the event of breakdown, there were no adequate means of transport, but only retreats, and, as we know, even on the Eastern Front, the rule was 'stationary tank, dead tank'. Photographic evidence shows that in some cases the help of a Breda 32 tractor from the 7th Road Rescue Unit of the 3rd Celere Division was invaluable. On the other hand, the units gave evidence of genuine valour several times, as in Africa, even though the chances of bringing home the bacon were slim.

The tanks highlighted a number of problems of a different nature and complexity.

One of the main difficulties reported on the Western Front was the difficulty of cold starting the engines of the L6/40 and L40 self-propelled vehicles. For this reason, a special pre-heating system was designed, consisting of a Paghetti hot-air generator, which was officially adopted at the beginning of December 1942. Weighing just over 350 kg, equipped with wheels and fuelled by diesel, through pipes with a shaped end to cover the cooling grids of the L6 tanks, the generator made it possible to bring the engines to a suitable temperature. It is not clear whether it was later switched to series production. A similar heater is still preserved in the Museo della Motorizzazione Militare at Cecchignola in Rome.

Also striking is the ease of failure of the infamous 'magnet snap joint'.

Finally, in the already mentioned report of Lieutenant Albanese of 6 September 1942, there are some notes on the tanks, particularly on the malfunctioning of the weapons:

"[...]

9. Radio: worked well.

10. Weapons: several machine gun and machine gun jams occurred, not due to a lack of cleaning or lubrication, but almost exclusively due to the failure to extract the cartridge case (steel for the 20-gauge and 8-gauge).

The extractor removed the butt pad, on which it was gripping, without extracting the cartridge case stuck in the chamber.

For the extraction of the cartridge case, the hand extractor often had to be used, resulting in a slower rate of fire. In some cases, the use of the ramrod introduced at the muzzle would also have been necessary.

[...]

The 20mm and 8mm rounds fired in Italy, with brass casings, have never given rise to such problems.

Slow movement of the turret, so the lack of a weapon in the tail was felt.

Inconvenient location of magazines and difficulty in extracting them from their housings.

In the case of the 8-calibre machine gun, the firing pin in beating against the capsule removed parts of it in the return, which, interposing themselves between the moving parts, caused some gun jamming'.

The Russians captured more than one, in various stages of efficiency and completeness, as early as the late summer of 1942, but it must not have impressed the Soviet engineers, in fact, only one has been preserved to this day, still in good condition. It has recently been restored at least to presentability, but repainted incorrectly.

Individual decorations awarded to military personnel of the department

Silver Medals for Military Valour
- Bartolucci Umberto, Major of the LXVII Armoured Bersaglieri Battalion.

Bronze Medal for Military Valour
- Masella Guido, Bersagliere of the LXVII Armoured Bersaglieri Battalion.

Military Cross for Valour
- Cossa Natale, Bersagliere of the LXVII Armoured Bersaglieri Battalion;
- Farina Raffaele, Bersagliere of the LXVII Armoured Bersaglieri Battalion;
- Trevisari Giuseppe, Bersagliere of the LXVII Armoured Bersaglieri Battalion;
- Trevisan Francesco, corporal of the LXVII Armoured Bersaglieri Battalion.

▲ L6/40 tanks of the XLVII Motorised Battalion on their way to Russia, on board a railway convoy. On the first tank on the left, one can see the tactical symbol of the 4th and 5th Platoon, in use exclusively at this Battalion, consisting of the coloured rectangle, on which a white crossbar was placed.

▼ The peculiar arrangement of the tactical markings and their non-standard size on the L6/40s of the XLVII Motorised Battalion bound for Russia is evident.

▲ On the inside of the side doors of each of the L6s of the Motorised Battalion, the name of a fallen soldier or fact of arms, related to the history of the Bersaglieri (in this case *'Regoldo'*), was indicated in black paint.

▼ The roads in Russia were often made impassable by mud, which became a real trap for motor vehicles.

▲ A FIAT 626 truck passes through a Russian village.

▼ A ceremony at the LXVII Motorised Bersaglieri Battalion in Russia, with tanks from the 1st Platoon of the 2nd Company. Note the larger markings than required by regulations (Castor).

▲ The commander of the XXXV Army Corps, General Messe, decorates some Italian soldiers for actions on the Don River front. In the foreground we can see a tank of the LXVII Bersaglieri Motorised Battalion (Grigoletti).

▲ Another picture of commander Giovanni Messe handing out field valour awards for actions on the Don front, in which the Bersaglieri with their L6/40 tanks also participated.

▼ The long-distance transport of the L6s of the Motocorazzato Battalion was carried out by FIAT 666 trucks, as can be seen in this picture.

▲ Plate by the talented draughtsman Piero Compagni, depicting a Bersagliere carrista of the XLVII Motorised Battalion during the Russian campaign.

▲ Sergeant Giorgio dell'Amico of the XLVII Motorised Battalion on his L6/04 tank, number plate 'RE 4050'. (D'Amico via Tallilllo)

COMANDO DEL II° CORPO D'ARMATA

------------------o------------------

ENCOMIO SOLENNE DI C. A.
==

~ valendomi delle facoltà confertemi dal n.536 del regolamento
di disciplina R.E., tributo un encomio solenne di C.A. (da
iscriversi)

al   Sergente   DELL'AMICO Giorgio di Michele

appartenente al   LXVVII° btg. bersaglieri corazzato

con la seguente motivazione:

"" SOTTUFICIALE RADIOTELEGRAFISTA, IN PRESENZA DI UNA INCUR-
SIONE DI CARRI ARMATI NEMICI, CHE AVEVANO GIA' AGGIRATA LA
POSIZIONE, VISTO IL CARRO COMANDO FERMO IN AVARIA, RIMANE-
VA IN POSTO PER RIMETTERLO IN EFFICIENZA.
MINACCIATO DALLE CRESCENTI OFFESE DEL NEMICO CONTINUAVA NEL
RISCHIOSO COMPITO FINO A QUANDO, RESO IMPOSSIBILE IL RICUPE-
RO ANCHE COL RIMORCHIO, DISTRUGGEVA GLI ORGANI VITALI DEL
CARRO E SI SOTTRAEVA ALLA CATTURA APRENDOSI IL VARCO ATTRA-
VERSO GLI ELEMENTI ESPLORANTI NEMICI, CATTURANDO PRIGIONIERI.
ESEMPIO DI TENACE VOLONTA' E DI SPREZZO DEL PERICOLO. ""

Gadjutschje (Russia) il 17 dicembre 1942/XXI

Zona di operazioni li?.....15 gennaio.......... 1943/XXI

                              IL GENERALE DI C.A. COMANDANTE
                                    (G. Zanghieri)

▲ The letter communicating the motivation for the Solemn Citation granted to Marconist Sergeant Dell'Amico, for his courageous behaviour on 18 December 1942, during the Battle of Gadjutscheye; after trying to repair his tank to continue the battle, he was forced to sabotage it.

▲ Group of Bersaglieri next to an L6/40 tank radio centre of the XLVII Motorised Battalion in Russia in 1942. The soldiers wear the turquoise jumpsuit, intended for tank crews, and on their tank helmets they proudly display the plumage that has always distinguished the Bersaglieri.

▼ The same tank as in the previous photo, portrayed as the crew consumes the ration. The sandy yellow colour of the vehicle and the tactical markings are clearly visible.

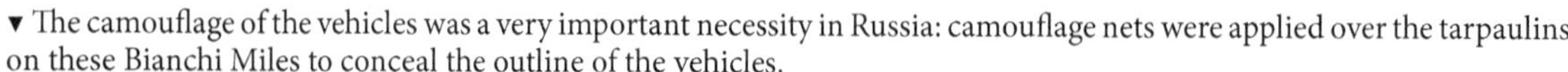

▲ The crew of an L6/40 poses next to their tank. (from the book 'Dalla Russia noi siamo tornati by Attilio Scolari)

▼ The camouflage of the vehicles was a very important necessity in Russia: camouflage nets were applied over the tarpaulins on these Bianchi Miles to conceal the outline of the vehicles.

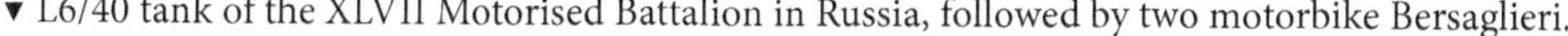

▲ The tanks also required ad hoc camouflage. On the L6 tanks of the XLVII Motorised Battalion, makeshift camouflage made of mud and, as in this case, branches was applied to further confuse the peculiar shapes of the vehicles.

▼ L6/40 tank of the XLVII Motorised Battalion in Russia, followed by two motorbike Bersaglieri.

▲ The L6/40s on the Russian front could not be engaged in engagements against enemy tanks, due to the obvious imbalance of forces, but only as infantry support.

▲ This photo allows us to appreciate the position of the tactical markings on the tanks of the XLVII Motorised Battalion, markings made in a larger than usual size.

▼ Deployment on the Eastern Front showed that the L6/40's engine had serious difficulties starting at low temperatures. The Società Piemontese Automobili tried to solve this problem by developing a pre-heating system, to which up to four L6 and L40 self-propelled tanks could be connected, by heating the engine compartment before starting the vehicle.

▲ The tank plate 'RE 3820' recovered from a truck on the Eastern Front (from the book *'Dalla Russia noi siamo tornati'* by Attilio Solari).

▼ This L6/40 has incomplete camouflage over the entire hull and, like the other tanks of the 2nd Company, hoists a tricolour pennant on the antenna (Fuscalzo).

▲ L6/40 column of the LVXII Motorised Bersaglieri Battalion marching in the summer of 1942 (Fuscalzo).

▼ This photo of an L6/40, taken from the back, shows the layout of the tactical markings on the hatch at the rear of the turret.

▲ A group of Alpini observe a column formed by some L640s of the LXVII Armoured Bersaglieri Battalion on the Eastern Front.

▼ An L6/40 tank of the LVXII Bersaglieri Battalion boards a FIAT 666 truck for long-distance transport.

▲ Soviet prisoners and captured automatic weapons in front of an L6/04 tank of the LVXII Bersaglieri Battalion, which supported Alpine units in Jagodnij in 1942.

▼ A Russian infantryman, armed with the 1941 model Degtyarev counter-tank gun (PTRD), 14.5 mm calibre, pictured in front of the captured 'RE 3882' tank in September 1942.

▲ Russian soldiers of the 38th Rifle Regiment of the 14th Guards Division observe two L6/40 tanks, captured during the battle of 1 September 1942 west of Bolschoj, as also recounted in the report of Lieutenant Albanese, commander of the 2nd Tank Company, quoted in the text.

▼ Tanks of the 5th Platoon of the 1st Company of the LVXII Bersaglieri Battalion, photographed on 2 October 1942. The L6/40 tank in the foreground has the number plate 'RE 3844'; note the mottled camouflage colouring, probably green (Castor).

XIII SELF-PROPELLED SQUADRON GROUP 'CAVALRY OF ALEXANDRIA'

In the period from 1940 to 1943, two Coastal Squadron Groups (XII and XIII), which operated in Italy, two Tank Squadron Groups (III and IV), equipped with L6/40 light tanks, were set up at the regimental depot of the 14th Regiment *Cavalry of Alexandria*, equipped with L6/40 light tanks, which were deployed to the Balkans, one Self-propelled Squadron Group (the XIII) with three L40 47/32 self-propelled squadrons, which was sent to Russia in 1942 and one Road Movement Battalion (the XII) which was sent to North Africa

In August 1942, the 13th Self-propelled Squadron Group *Cavalry of Alexandria* also reached the Russian front. The Group was organised on:

- Command
- Command Squadron
- 1st Self-Propelled Squadron
- 2nd Self-Propelled Squadron

with a total of 19 self-propelled 47/32 L40s, intended to provide supporting fire for the Infantry and L6/40 tanks of the LXVII Bersaglieri Battalion. The latter was withdrawn to the rear in November for a reorganisation phase. At the beginning of the winter, the Battalion and the XIII Self-propelled Group passed to the 3rd Celere P.A.D.A. Division and then to the II Army Corps.

In the following month of December, the sector of the Italian front held by the 'Cosseria' and *'Ravenna'* Divisions suffered a violent Russian attack and on 11 December, the two armoured divisions were recalled into the line, reinforcing the positions held by the two Italian Divisions and some German divisions. Despite the strenuous Italian resistance, between 16th and 21st December, the Soviets broke through the defensive line of the *"Ravenna"*, between Gadjucja and Filonovo , and already on the 19th, the Italian divisions had to start retreating. The Bersaglieri of the LXVII Armoured Battalion and the Light Cavalry of the XIII Self-Propelled Squadron Group had the task of covering the retreat with the few surviving armoured vehicles from the clashes of the previous days (about twenty in all); most of these tanks and self-propelled vehicles were lost during the retreat, which ended on 28 December at Skassirskaja. The very few remaining armoured tanks were then dispersed in the disastrous retreat of the A. R. M. I. R.

Some L6 and 47/32 self-propelled vehicles, captured by Soviet troops, were kept for a few years (e.g. an L40 self-propelled vehicle was exhibited in 1947 in Moscow's Gorky Park, together with other armoured vehicles captured from the enemy, as evidenced by some photographs, but was later demolished).

Individual decorations awarded to military personnel of the department

Military Cross for Valour
- Arbitrio Michele, cavalryman of the XIII Group of Self-propelled Squadrons *'Cavalry of Alexandria'*.
-

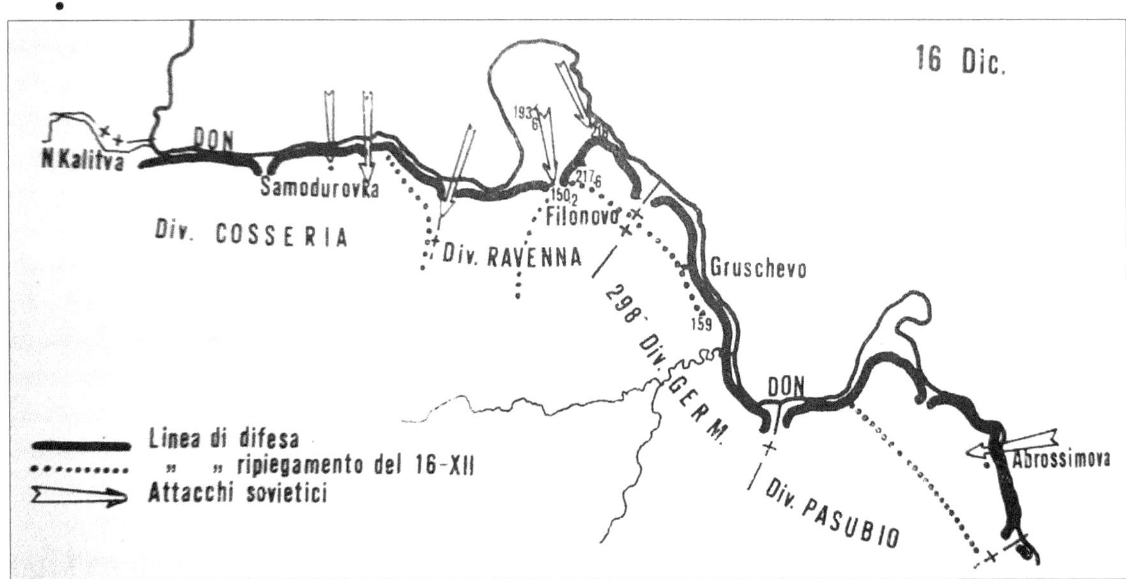

▲ Soviet attack on the defensive line of the Don, held by the Italian *'Cosseria'*, *'Ravenna'* and *'Pasubio'* Divisions and the German 298th Division, on 16 December 1942. The front gave way in the sector held by the *'Ravenna'* Division between Gadjucja and Filonovo. The Bersaglieri of the LXVII Armoured Battalion and the Cavalry of the XIII Group of Self-propelled Squadrons had to cover the retreat with the few surviving armoured vehicles.

▼ Uniform of a captain of the *'Cavalry of Alexandria'*.

▲ Two 47/32 L40 self-propelled vehicles of the XIII Gruppo Squadroni Semoventi *'Cavalry of Alexandria'* trudge through the snow and the terrain made muddy by the weather in the late autumn of 1942. The vehicles bear mottled camouflage and the first self-propelled vehicle has a horseshoe fixed on the front shield, probably as a good luck charm (from the book *'Dalla Russia noi siamo tornati'* by Attilio Solari).

▼ The fearsome 'General Winter', which had already given Napoleon a hard time, once again proved to be an invincible enemy. Pictured, left, a FIAT 666 truck.

▲ The Soviet winter offensives, which began in late 1942, gradually overwhelmed the A.R.M.I.R. The armoured units of the Regio Esercito also paid the price. This L6/40 of the LVXXI Bersaglieri Motorised Battalion destroyed by enemy fire clearly shows an extemporaneous winter camouflage. (Leonardo Landi)

▲ The same tank from the previous photo, taken from another angle, being observed by an intrigued Soviet infantryman.

▲ Painful image of death and destruction featuring an L6/40 and an Italian soldier.

▲ Another sad image of the Italian defeat: some Russian soldiers advance on the positions abandoned by the Italians. (Leonardo Landi)

▼ A Pavesi tractor tows a stalled Lancia 3 Ro, followed by another Pavesi.

▲ Soviet riflemen marched alongside the L6/40 tank, plate 'RE 3879', and overtook it. (Leonardo Landi)

▼ More tanks of the LVXXI Motorised Bersaglieri Battalion abandoned among the isbas in the same village as the previous pictures: one can see the field camouflage colouring, created in an attempt to disguise the armoured vehicles in the freezing Russian winter. (Leonardo Landi)

▲ Italian vehicles destroyed during the retreat from the Voronezh front in January 1943.

▼ A FIAT 666 truck and TL37 artillery tractors abandoned during the Voronezh retreat. Next to the vehicles, piles of frozen corpses.

▲ Another image that gives the measure of the Italian-German route on the Voronezh front in January 1943.

▼ A TL37 tractor with its artillery piece still in tow, hit and blocked by enemy shots.

▲ Some artillerymen try to rescue themselves aboard a TM40 in poor condition, but still running.

▼ Behind the FIAT 626 truck in the foreground can be seen a 47/32 L40 self-propelled vehicle of the XIII Gruppo Squadroni Semoventi *'Cavalry of Alexandria'*.

▲ In the snowy expanse of the Russian steppe lay many Italian vehicles that had been lost during the retreat of December 1942, a consequence of the Russian breakthrough on 19 December. Among the carcasses were two L6/40 tanks of the LXVII Bersaglieri Battalion and a 47/32 self-propelled tank of the *'Cavalry of Alexandria'*.

▼ Two L6/40 tanks of the LXVII Motorised Battalion put out of action: on the front of the tank in the foreground, that of Sergeant Giorgio dell'Amico, plate 'RE 4050', the inscription 'LXVII' can be seen, not found on other tanks of the same Battalion.

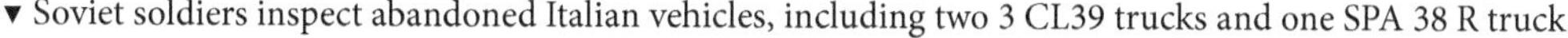

▲ L6/40 tanks of the LXVII Motorised Bersaglieri Battalion put out of action. The white camouflage colouring, made with washable paint, is interesting. (Leonardo Landi)

▼ Soviet soldiers inspect abandoned Italian vehicles, including two 3 CL39 trucks and one SPA 38 R truck.

▲ L6/40 of the LXVII Battalion Bersaglieri Motocorazzato plate number 'RE 3898', exhibited in 1944 at the NIBT balipedium in Kubinka.

▲ The same tank seen from the side: the tactical markings indicate that it was the fourth tank of the 1st Platoon of the 1st Company.

▼ L6/40 of the LXVII Motorised Battalion survived the war and was exhibited in Russia together with other armoured vehicles. The tank has the number plate 'RE 3912' and bears the markings of the 3rd Platoon tank of the 1st Company.

▲ The L6/40 tank of the LXVII Motorised Battalion stored in Russia at the Armoured Troops Museum in Kubinka, depicted in poor condition; it is the same tank as the previous photo.

▼ The preserved tank in Kubinka, after a conservative restoration it underwent. Some of the details are postictive, such as the armament, while the track suspension is now completely worn out.

▲ Next to the L6/40 is a Hungarian L3/35, also of war vintage, repainted in a rather fanciful pattern, on which Italian tactical symbols have been affixed.

▼ The two tanks photographed next to each other.

▲ The Hungarian L3/35 tank is a command model, recognisable by the modified hood of the foreman.

▼ The last surviving L6/40 tank of the LXVII Motorised Bersaglieri Battalion, still preserved in the large Russian museum in Kubinka, restored in 2018, although not properly.

'NIZZA CAVALRY' ARMOURED CAR PLATOON OF THE 'VICENZA' INFANTRY DIVISION

In September 1942, the *'Vicenza'* Infantry Division was destined for the Russian front, following the A.R.M.I.R. and, for the large unit, a 'territorial' deployment behind the rear was planned. For this reason, the 156th Artillery Regiment was detached from the divisional staff, inserting in its place the XXVI Battaglione mobilised Carabinieri Reali from Bologna and an Autoblindo Platoon, equipped with 2 AB41s and 9 men. On 22 July, an urgent request was made for the establishment of an Autoblindo Platoon at the 1st 'Nizza Cavalry' Regiment in Turin, which was to be set up by 20 August.

In October of the same year, the transfer of the Division to Russia began and the Platoon followed the unit on the long journey to the enemy: '[...] *from Pinerolo, at the Cavalry School, it began with an interminable journey by train-train, three thousand kilometres, through Italy, Austria and Czechoslovakia, until it reached the Ukraine*'[4].

On 24 December 1942, the Autoblindo Platoon was de facto hived off from the *'Vicenza'* Division, coming under the direct command of the 8th Army, together with the XXVI Battalion mobilised Royal Carabinieri.

Unfortunately, there is no news of either the Platoon's operational deployment or what happened to it during the disastrous retreat from the Don. From the aforementioned memoirs of the transmitter engineer Eugène Lanteri-Minet, we only learn that one of the two AB41s broke down during the long retreat and was towed by the other armoured car to Minsk, where the surviving units of the *'Vicenza'* gathered. Here, the two armoured cars were commandeered by the Germans, before the Italian soldiers returned to Italy. During the entire Russian campaign, the Autoblindo Platoon recorded no casualties.

According to the documentation of the Royal Army[5], on the date of the disbandment of the Division (2 May 1943), the Autoblindo Platoon was still in charge of the *'Vicenza'*, with 2 machines and 9 men, and the demobilisation of the Platoon was entrusted to the *'Nizza Cavalry'* Regiment Depot.

---

4 Testimony of the transmitter engineer Eugène Lanteri-Minet, a member of the AB41 crew of the *'Nizza Cavalry'*, who survived the great retreat of 1943, reported on the website www.divisionevicenza.it.

5 'Demobilisation and disbandment of the Infantry Division *"Vicenza"* (256)', 2 May 1943, Carabinieri Historical Archives.

▲ Royal Army soldiers inspect a destroyed Soviet BT-5.

▼ A series of unpublished photographs of destroyed or captured Soviet armoured vehicles taken by an officer of the *'Savoia Cavalry'* Regiment during the Russian campaign: in this image, a Red Army T-37A amphibious light tank (Lucchetti).

ARMOURED VEHICLES OF
WARLIKE PREY

Between 1941 and 1942, the CSIR (and later the ARMIR) managed to capture a number of enemy armoured vehicles (probably a total of 14 tanks and 2 armoured cars), which were re-deployed by units of the Regio Esercito. Among the captured vehicles were a T 37A amphibious light tank, two BT 7 M, at least one T 60, one T 26 Mod. 39 and two T 34 medium tanks (one Mod. 39 and one Mod. 41 / 42 Stz).

The subjects on which there is most documentation are undoubtedly the T 34s. One of these, the Model 39 (which is unclear whether it was actually captured by the Italians or more likely given away by the Germans) was taken to the Centro Studi della Motorizzazione in Rome and used for some evaluations. It was then returned to Germany just after 8 September 1943. The other was used by the LII Group of the 120th Artillery Regiment of the 3rd Celere Division as a command tank. The latter was most likely a vehicle abandoned by the Soviets due to mechanical failure and the Italian artillerymen managed to get it back in running condition. In order to identify it and avoid being the target of friendly fire, several white crosses were applied (two on the two sides, a larger one at the rear and a smaller one on the front shield of the gun, and a very large one on the turret top, on the crew hatch). At another time, white sheets were used for aerial recognition. The tank was the protagonist of a Luce newsreel filmed on the occasion of the visit of General Italo Gariboldi, Commander of the 8th Army of the Royal Army to the units of the Celere Division. He hoisted a tricolour for the occasion, attached to a makeshift pole secured to the inside of the turret hatch. Apparently, other T 34s, which did not work, were used as fixed targets to assess the effectiveness of the counter-tank pieces supplied to the Regio Esercito.

Of the various captured Soviet vehicles, the most interesting remain two BM 13 self-propelled rocket launchers (more commonly called *'Katiuscia'*). This weapon, which entered service in July 1941, was easier to manufacture than artillery pieces, so much so that over 3,200 were completed by the end of 1942. In addition, their volume of fire was very high.

The first of the two " Katiuscia" captured was on an English Austin K6 three-axle chassis (6 x 4), from Lend Lease and was recovered, damaged and missing two of its rear wheels, by Lieutenant Gastone Pocci of the 14th Artillery Specialists Department of the 8th Army, commanded by Captain Attilio Sartori and later by Lieutenant Colonel Geranzani. It was subjected to at least one employment demonstration at Migulinskaya in August 1942 and then used to protect the retreat of other Italian units, first in the Starobelsk area and then in the Kupiansk area from 20 December 1942 to 18 January 1943. Here it was sabotaged because it was now out of ammunition.

The other, which was also damaged, was on a Soviet Zis 6 chassis and was tested at Matcsewskaja in October 1942, moving it thanks to a TL 37 . There is also less information about its use, although its silhouette was chosen for a non-regulation frieze, which was made by the department tailor in about thirty pieces. A photograph of it appeared in an issue of the *'Corriere della Sera'* in May 1943.

▲ Lieutenant Lucchetti poses in front of a destroyed BA-6 heavy armoured car (Lucchetti).

▼ Next to this BA-20 armoured car lie the bodies of the crew members. A Lancia 3 RO truck of the Regio Esercito (Lucchetti) can be seen in the background.

▲ Infantryman of the *'Savoia Cavalry'* Regiment have their photo taken on a Soviet T-34 tank (Lucchetti).

▼ Artillerymen of the 62nd Group of the 120th Artillery Regiment show the Russian tank they captured, T-34/76B, to General Italo Gariboldi, Commander of the 8th Army of the Royal Army, on a visit to the units under his command.

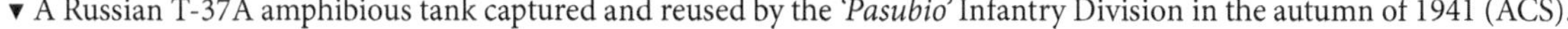

▲ Italian soldiers, armed with two Russian PTRD 41 anti-tank guns, pose with a Soviet T-60 tank put out of action in Ukraine in the summer of 1941.

▼ A Russian T-37A amphibious tank captured and reused by the *'Pasubio'* Infantry Division in the autumn of 1941 (ACS).

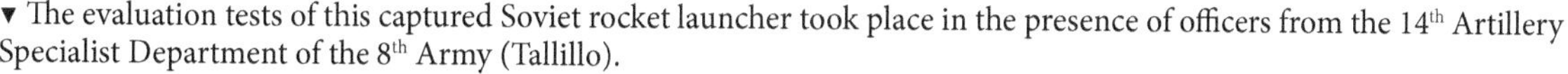

▲ A BM 13 *'Katiuscia'* self-propelled rocket launcher on a Soviet Zis 6 chassis, towed by a TL37. The image refers to experimental trials conducted Matcsewskaja in October 1942 (Tallillo).

▼ The evaluation tests of this captured Soviet rocket launcher took place in the presence of officers from the 14th Artillery Specialist Department of the 8th Army (Tallillo).

▲ Artillerymen of the 14th Artillery Specialist Division of the 8th Army engaged in loading the heavy shells of the *'Katiuscia'* (Tallillo).

▼ Detail of the launch pad of the BM 13 *'Katiuscia'* self-propelled rocket launcher on a Soviet Zis 6 (Tallillo) chassis.

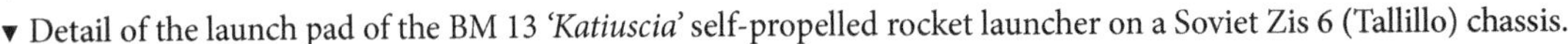

▲ Reproduction of the special frieze of the 14th Artillery Specialists Division of the 8th Army deployed in Russia (Tallillo).

▼ Profile reproducing the BM 13 *'Katiuscia'* self-propelled rocket launcher on an Austin K chassis: an example of this model was also captured by the Italians and used in combat (Tallillo).

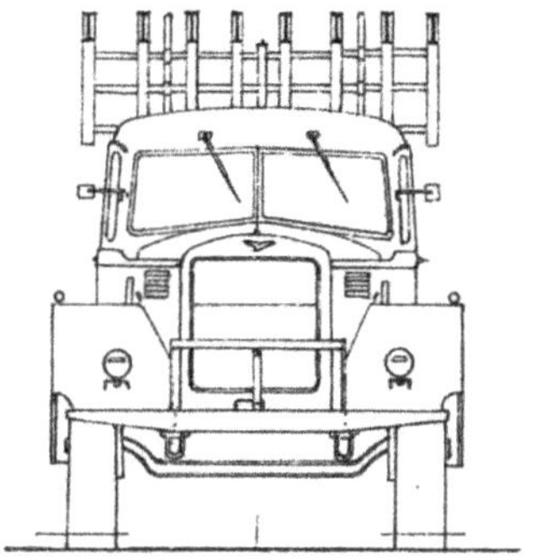

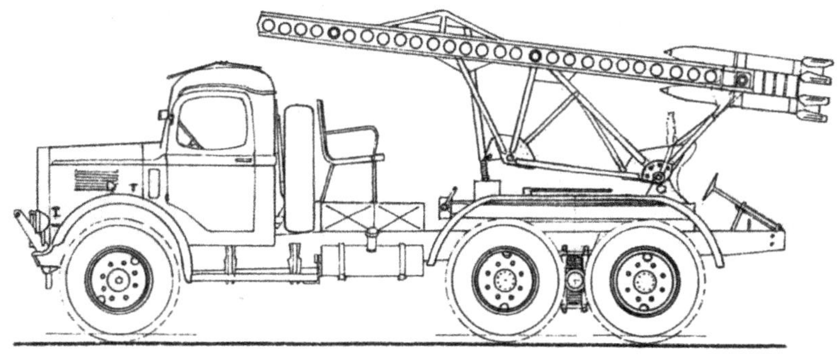

▲ Soviet T-34/76A tank during evaluation tests held in Rome at the Centro Studi della Motorizzazione.

▼ The T-34 tested in Italy for some time, which was then 'returned' after 8 September to the Germans (Tallillo).

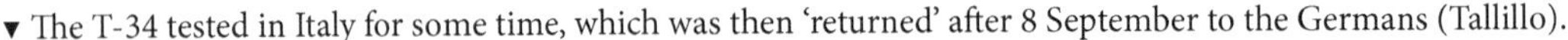

THE ARDITI OF THE 'PARIS' GROUP

In May 1943, there were two Battalions of the 'Young Fascists' Regiment in Italy, the XI, composed of young veterans from the African front, repatriated due to wounds or illness, and the VI. The Regiment was officially disbanded following the fall of the Duce and the soldiers of the unit were allowed to transfer to the X Arditi Regiment or other units. The Armistice took the X Arditi by surprise and it was, in fact, disbanded by the Command; the Young Fascists, in the general disbandment, left the Santa Severa headquarters for the capital, in the hope of meeting some other unit determined not to give in to the armistice clauses. Arriving in Rome on 18 September, the Camionettisti got in touch with the 2nd Fallschirmjäger Division *'Ramke'* and managed to get themselves accepted as one of the unit's members. This consisted of about 300 volunteers from the 112th Trucker Company of the 2nd Battalion of the 10th, commanded by Captain Paolo Paris, and the 133rd Company, but also other soldiers from the newly formed Parachute Division 'Cyclone'. At first, the Young Fascists were employed to maintain public order in the City and to guard the E.I.A.R. headquarters. guaranteeing the functioning of the radio station. The entire Division moved to Castel di Decima, at the royal estate of Castel Porziano, outside Rome, where the staff was supplemented by other Arditi and Young Fascists. A total of 107 Young Fascists voluntarily followed the fate of the 'Ramcke'. The Italian soldiers were then divided into two groups, one of which, under the command of Captain Paris, consisted of about fifty Arditi with a complement of 6 metropolitan model AS trucks, and this group was framed in the German Division as a scouting unit with the name *'Gruppo Arditi Camionettisti Italiani'*. The Group, under the command of Captain Paris, was organised into two sections, each of which was assigned a German lieutenant to act as interpreter. The Italian soldiers continued to wear their Arditi uniforms, which were gradually supplemented with Luftwaffe clothing as needed, while proudly retaining, alongside the German ranks and insignia, the Arditi frieze on the left sleeve and the Young Fascists' badge on the chest, by concession of the Division Command.

During the month of October, the Group underwent an intensive training cycle, carried out at divisional level and according to German standards, and at the end of October, the *'Ramke'* was assigned to the Eastern Front. The transfer of the Division began and the Arditi then had to make a long and exhausting journey by rail, trucks in tow, slowed down by the poor condition of the rail network and the frequent Allied bombardments, arriving at their destination only in mid-November.

Arriving in the U.S.S.R. at Zhitomir in mid-November, the unit sustained its first combat forty kilometres from Kiev at the end of the month; the Camionettisti had in the meantime been divided between four Companies of the Division, thus ceasing to operate as an organic unit. Over the next few days, while deployed against Tatar and Mongol troops, there were the first Italian casualties and at least a couple of AS42 trucks, which had been used between rearguards and during some counter-attacks, were destroyed. Hard fighting ensued in the area of the Dnjestr river, which caused the first deaths among the truck drivers. We remember this bloody episode, in the course of which the commander of the truck drivers was killed. On 27 December 1943, under the command of Captain Paris, a group of 24 Arditi were sent to reach a group of three self-propelled vehicles that had become stranded in front of the Russian lines and to rescue the vehicles and crews. The Russian artillery, alerted, began to hammer the positions occupied by the Italians with an infernal fire, who only desisted from continuing the operation as their ammunition ran out. Having returned to their lines, the Italian Arditi resupplied themselves with ammunition and explosives and went on the attack again, clashing with the Soviet patrols that were regaining their positions near the self-propelled vehicles. The battle took place at gunpoint and ended with the defeat of the enemy, who left several dead and wounded on the ground. The losses of the Italian paratroopers were also high, and among the fallen was Captain Paris himself, who was proposed by the RSI Minister of Defence, Marshal Graziani, for the highest decoration for military valour. At the end of 1943, the *'Ramke'* Division, in support of Heer and SS armoured divisions, sustained further terrible battles and fell back to Romania. The paratroopers and the Arditi continued to fight throughout the retreat, losing all their trucks. These vehicles, which had been created for movement warfare in desert areas, were put to the test by terrain different from what they were born for and adverse weather conditions, but nevertheless gave a good account of themselves and proved to be a good product of Italian industry. In May 1944, thanks to the arrival of reinforcement troops, the remnants of the 2nd Fallshirmjager Division were sent to the vicinity of Cologne to reorganise. The valiant behaviour of the Fallshirmjager Division, who managed to rejoin their comrades in Romania, earned them a bonus leave, which only those living in areas not yet occupied by the Anglo-Americans could enjoy. On 13 June, the Division was transferred to France and sent to Normandy, to stem the overpowering tide of the Allies who had landed a few days earlier. It was thus deployed in bloody fighting, during which many Camionnaires lost their lives, first in the area of Carhaix and then at Landerneau and the Monts d'Arre. The Division, pressed by the Anglo-American advance, fell back to the stronghold of Brest, where it ceased resistance on 20 September 1944, surrendering to the Americans. For the surviving Comrades, the gates of imprisonment on British soil thus opened, returning to their homeland almost two years later. The Arditi di Paris left 18 comrades on the battlefields and had 26 wounded, 5 of whom were repatriated to Italy due to the serious wounds sustained in the fighting.

▲ One of the 'Metropolitan' type trucks of the *'Paris'* Group in the Ukraine, where the machines proved their reliability even in the cold Russian winter, despite the fact that they were designed for use in far less severe climates (Arena).

▲ An AS42 Metropolitana truck of the 10th Arditi Regiment surrounded by German paratroopers on 18 September 1943, when about 300 soldiers of the Regiment reached the Capital and managed to join the 2. Fallshirmjäger-Division *'Ramke'*. It is probably a command vehicle, because it is armed only with an 8 mm machine gun; the photo also shows the camouflage colouring of the vehicle and the number plate 'RE 1192B'. A large picture with a photograph of Mussolini (B.A.) was placed on the bonnet of the car, above the spare wheel housing.

▼ A second lieutenant of the 10th Armoured Regiment argues with an officer and some German paratroopers of the 2nd Fallshirmjäger-Division *'Ramke'* (B.A.).

▲ At the end of September, beginning of October 1943, the Arditi Camionettisti, after joining the German 2. Fallshirmjäger-Division *'Ramke'*, took part in an exercise in the Albani Hills in concert with the 242. One of the trucks heavily camouflaged with branches (Fallaok F1675 L37 - Werner Röpke- ECPAD - Défense).

▼ Another truck of the Arditi, note the lack of the container and jerry-cans on the right side of the vehicle (Fallaok F1675 L37 - Werner Röpke- ECPAD - Défense).

▲ An AS42 truck of the 'Paris' Group at Shitomir in Ukraine: the original three-tone camouflage can still be seen. The Arditi wore a mixture of Italian and German uniforms, but were allowed to use their own national badges (Arena).

▼ The same truck as in the previous photograph, taken on a snowy road. The 2nd Fallshirmjager Division was part of the XL Pz. Kps. (Arena).

▲ General Ramke talks with some Arditi of the Paris Group, during the campaign on Ukrainian soil (Arena).

▼ Another group of Italians on duty with the *'Ramke'* division, on board the 'RE 1204B' truck. The German command had words of great respect for the valour shown by this handful of Italian volunteers (Arena).

COLOURING OF ARMOURED VEHICLES

For the eastern front, no special distinguishing marks were used on the armoured vehicles, but those already in regular use were retained; the same can be said for the colouring of the vehicles, no special camouflage schemes were adopted, but only the LXVII Bersaglieri Battalion used field devices.

III Armoured Squadron Group *'San Giorgio'*

The L3 tanks of the *'San Giorgio'* Group reached Russian soil with the colouring they had at home, green or with small green patches on a rust-brown background.

LXVII Bersaglieri Battalion

The L6/40s of the LXVII Bersaglieri Battalion retained the standard sand yellow livery. Even before the end of the summer period, in order to make up for the lack of camouflage, the Bersaglieri applied a striking camouflage in irregular patches, made of mud, which often also covered the tank insignia and number plates. During the harsh Russian winter, some L6/40s were given an impromptu white camouflage colour scheme, made in a completely artisanal manner with white washable paint, which, however, tended to soon peel off or fade due to weathering or wear. This camouflage was sometimes unintentionally supplemented by natural camouflage due to ice and snow being deposited on the armour. In some photographs of tanks of the 5th Platoon of the 1st Company, a mottled camouflage, probably green, is detectable.

Tactical markings larger than usual and in different positions from the regular prescriptions (on the sides and rear of the turret, filling the entire length of the hatch, and on the front of the casemate) were applied to the tanks of the department and, in addition, there were also markings for 4th and 5th Platoon, which also implied a transverse bar, which was more unique than rare. The 5th Platoon was identified by a transverse bar on the rectangles, among other things arranged, on some tanks, differently according to the side of the vehicle. The position of the tank within the Platoon was identified by an Arabic number, always red, regardless of the Platoon, placed not above, but in front of the rectangle; on the commander's tank, the Roman number of the Battalion was in black, 10 cm high and carried on the front rectangle of the casemate and in front of the symbols in the turret. Other exceptions were, on tank number 3882, from a close examination of the remaining photographs, an attempt to paint the rectangles on the sides of the superstructure as well, and on another tank the presence of rectangles in the standard, but with the individual number in the typical Battalion position. Apart from these minor differences, the rest was quite normal, such as the black rectangles for the Command Platoon, while some details remained peculiar to L6 hulls such as the front number plate. It was divided into two blocks due to the presence of the towing eye in the middle of the vertical hull plate. Seen from the front, L6 tanks and self-propelled vehicles bore on the left the initials of the Regio Esercito and a red grenade, and on the right the actual number, of four digits. The department plates, as far as we could tell from examining various photographs, ranged from number 3812 to 4062. On the inclined bow plate was fixed the regular circular metal badge of belonging to the Regio Esercito. The white disc for aerial identification was present on the original livery but was probably also hidden with mud like the other markings, although to a lesser extent.

On the inside of the side doors of the L6 Battalion's tanks, the name of a fallen soldier or fact of arms, linked to the history of the Bersaglieri, was written in black. Finally, the tanks of the 2nd Company adopted a small tricolour, hoisted on the antenna.

XIII Self-propelled Squadron Group *'Cavalry of Alexandria'*

The self-propelled vehicles of the *'Cavalry of Alexandria'* adopted the mottled camouflage typical of the period and bore the standard tactical symbols on the sides of the casemate and on the back of the hull.

'Nizza Cavalry' Armoured Car Platoon of the *'Vicenza'* Infantry Division

There are no known pictures of the AB41 armoured cars of the *'Nizza Cavalry'* Armoured Platoon, so it is not possible to give any indication of their colouring.

'Paris' Group

The Paris Group's trucks, all of the so-called 'Metropolitan' model, retained the three-tone camouflage colouring and the original number plates, which were deprived of the 'RE' initials (the numbers '1197B' and '1204B' are known).

DRAWINGS – PROFILES – MARKINGS AND IMAGE GALLERIES

MARKINGS - TYPE LXVII BATTALION

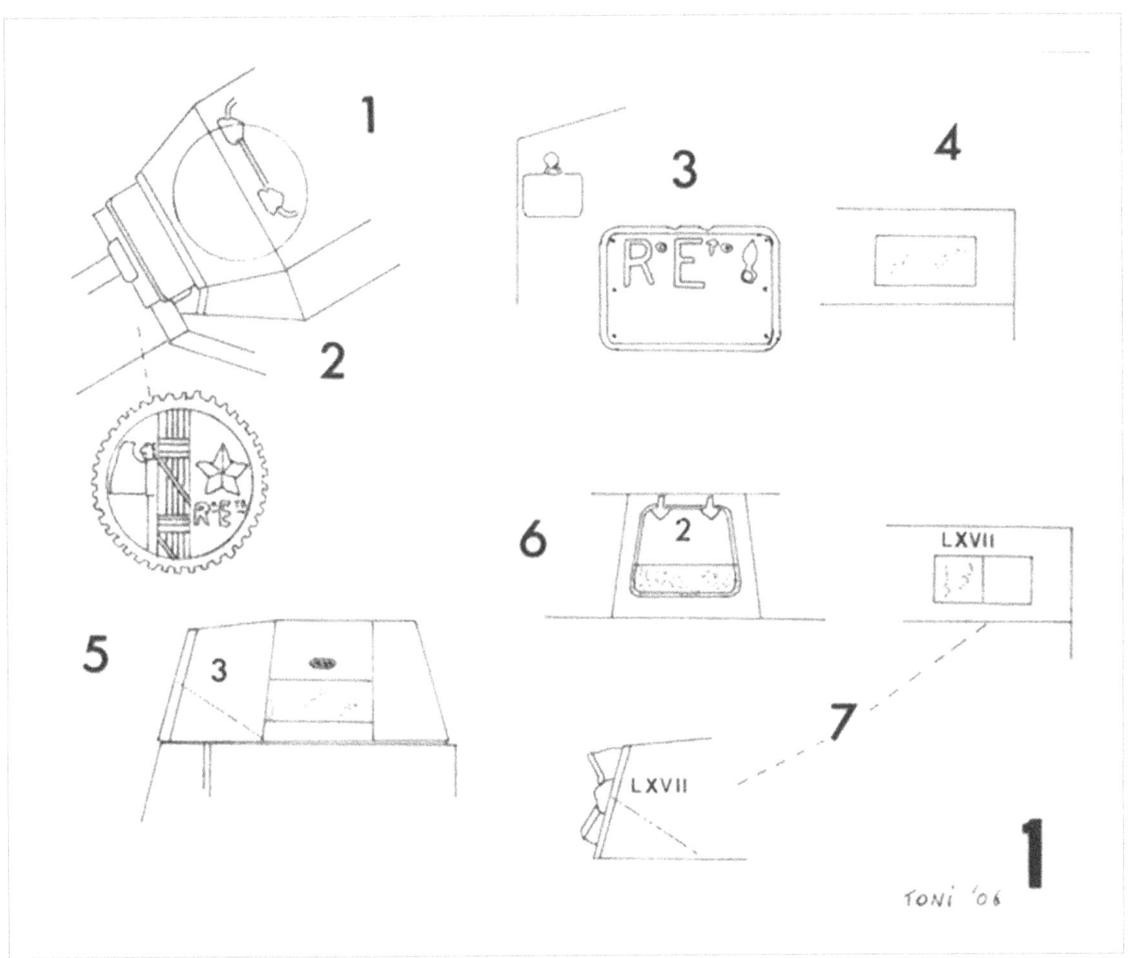

▲ 1 - Position aerial identification mark
  2 - Circular metal crest for RE armour
  3 - Rear plate position
  4 - Front position tactical mark on L6
  5 - Side mark
  6 - Rear mark
  7 - Tank mark LXVII Battalion commander

▲ 1 - Bersagliere in suit and jacket, ration officer. 2 - Sergeant, in suit model 26, tank commander. 3 - Tank of the 2nd Company, which was distinguished by its small flags (others had a small tricolour at the top (3A) and at least one those of the three Tripartite countries) (from CMPR)

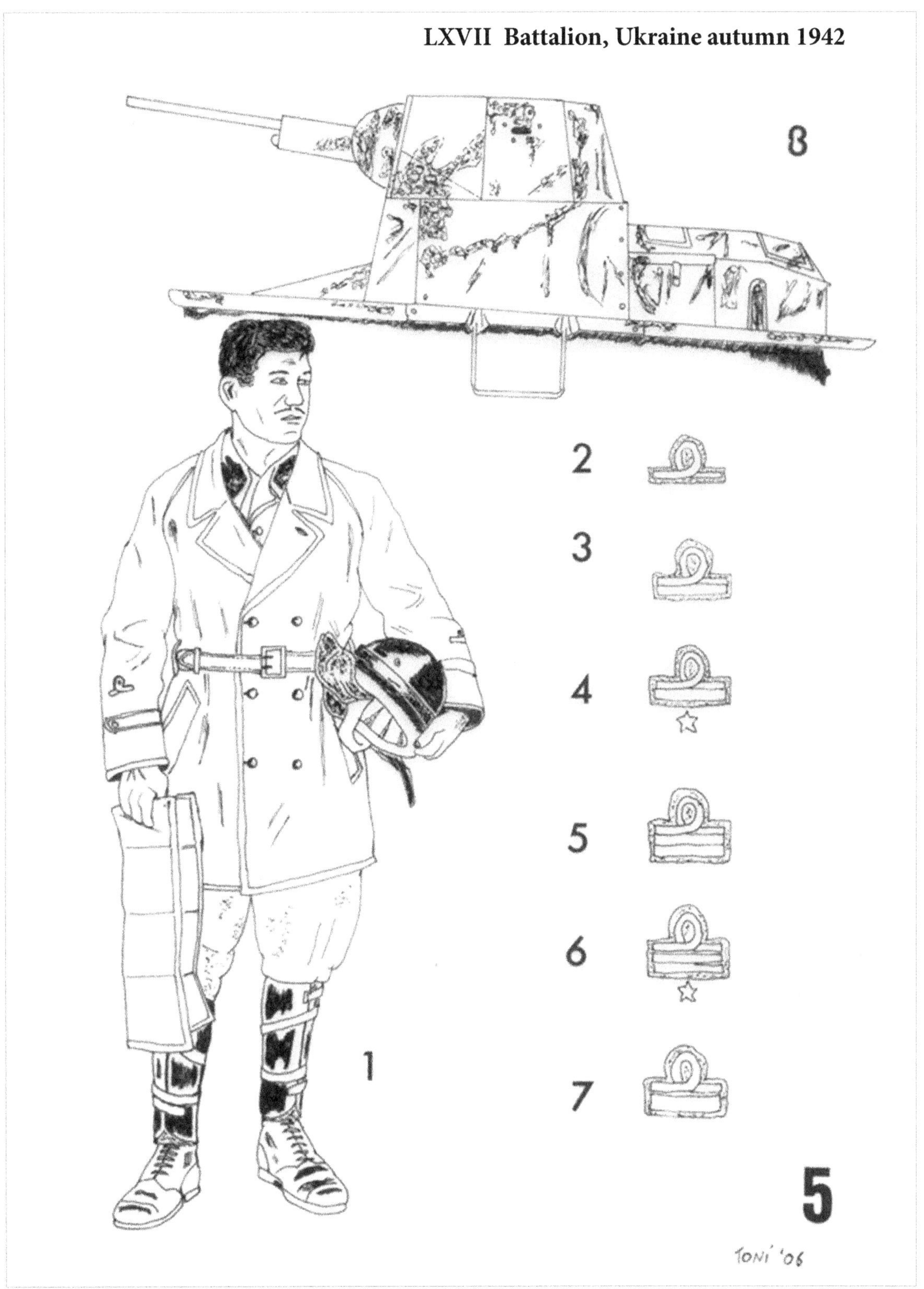

▲ 1 - Second Lieutenant in jacket and service uniform. 2 - Forearm rank, Second Lieutenant. 3 - Lieutenant. 4 - First Lieutenant. 5 - Captain. 6 - First Captain. 7 - Major. 8 - Battalion tank with the adopted extemporaneous camouflage (mud on base colour) (from CMPR)

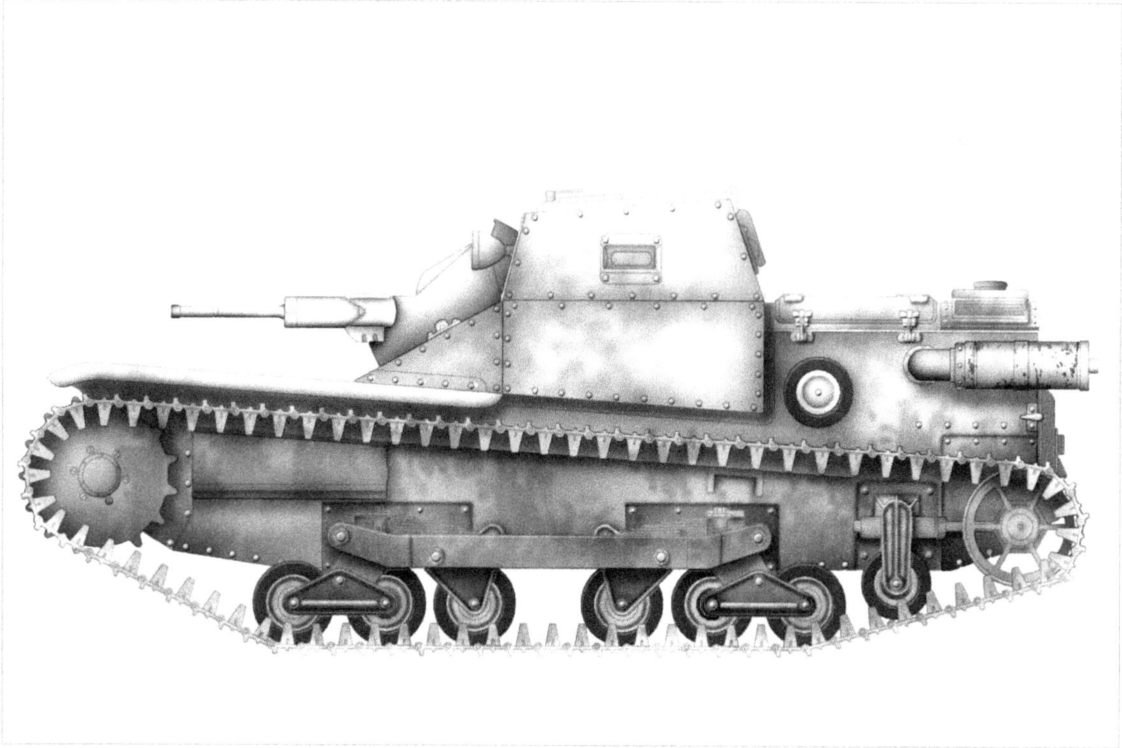

▲ Profile of light fast tanks of the type used in Russia. Drawings by Luca Cristini.

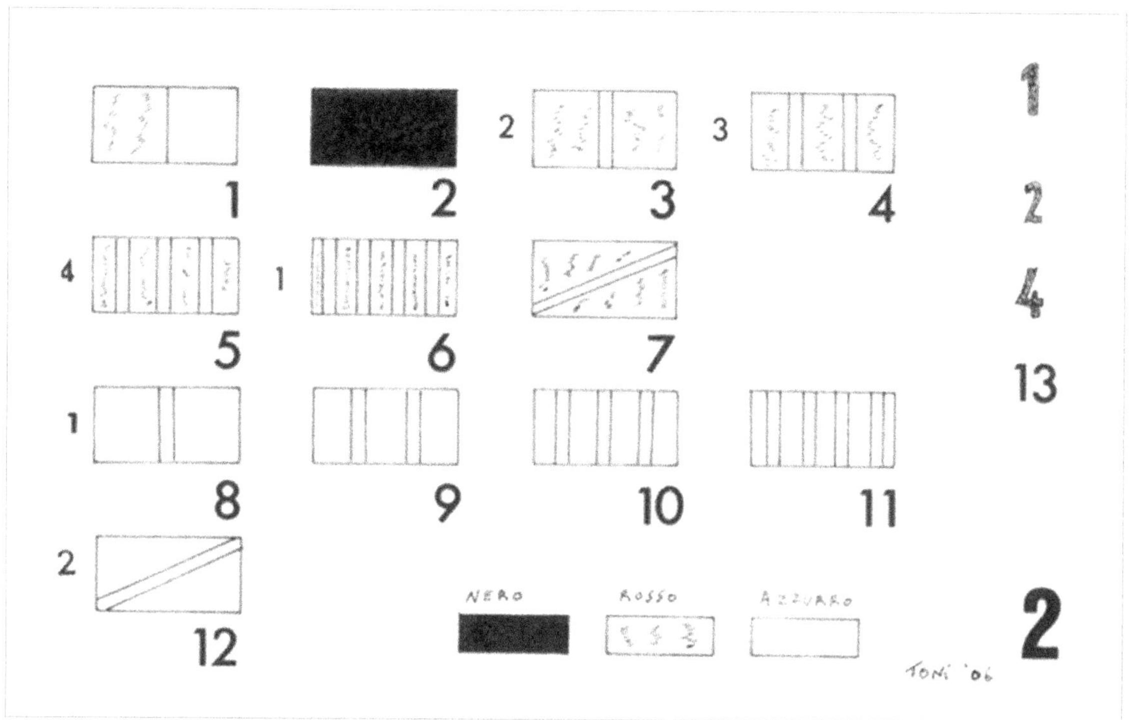

▲ 1 - Battalion Commander (licence plate 4050)

2 - Command Platoon (licence plate 4051) - Units 2 (licence plate 3896) and 3 (4061) were 'Radio Centre' tanks

3 - First Platoon, 1st Company (3820)

4 - Second Platoon (3844)

5 - Third Platoon (3917)

6 - Fourth Platoon (3882)

7 - Fifth platoon

8 - First platoon, 2nd Company (3830)

9 - Second Platoon

10 - Third platoon

11 - Fourth platoon

12 - Fifth platoon (4053)

13 - Some numbers

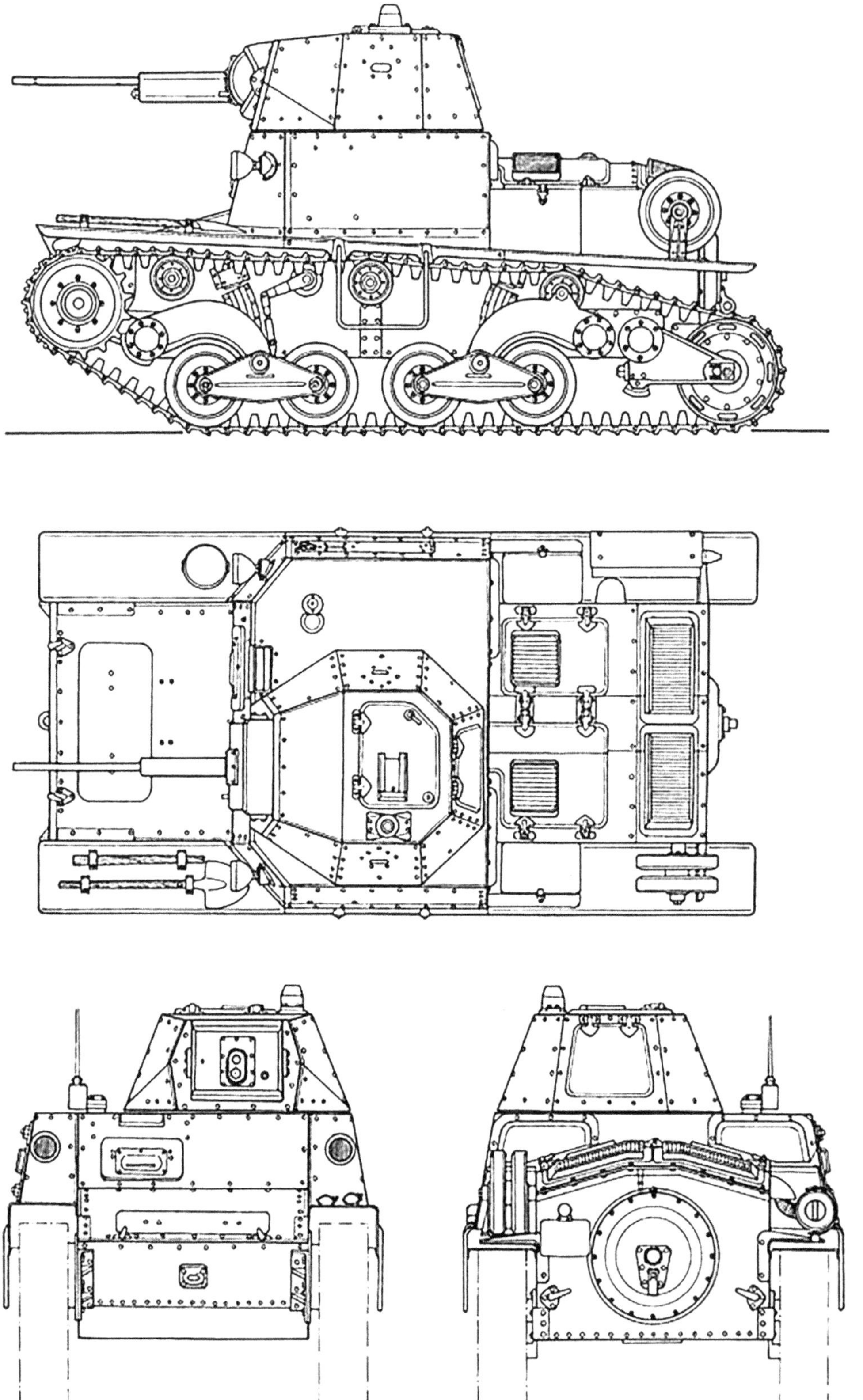

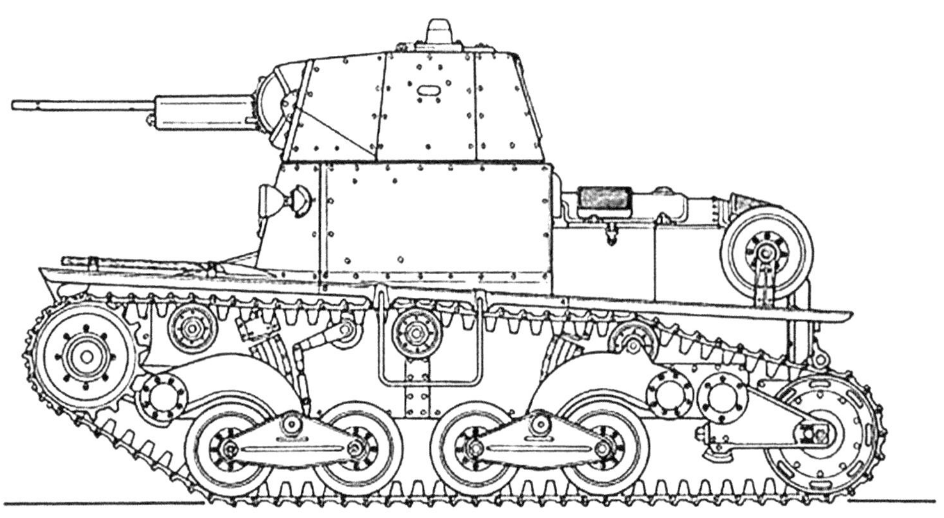

▲ Complete profile on 4 views from drawings by Ciuffoletti.

IMAGE GALLERY OF THE L6/40 TANK OF THE LXVIII BERSAGLIERI BATTALION PRESERVED IN THE RUSSIAN MUSEUM IN KUBINKA (SOURCE CMPR)

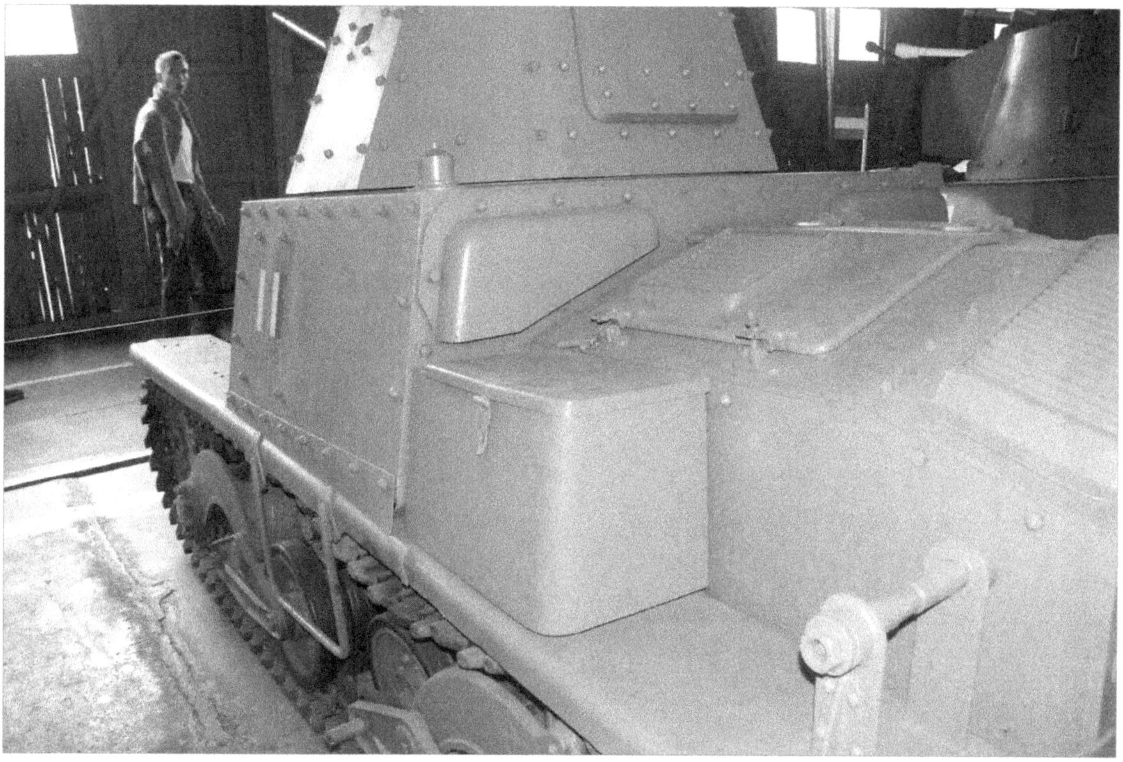

The tank unit, presumably RE 3912, third platoon of the 1st Company, of the three existing in the world is the best preserved. Photo by Mr. Boris Kharlamov in Kubinka (via U. Plinkner and S. Sogni).

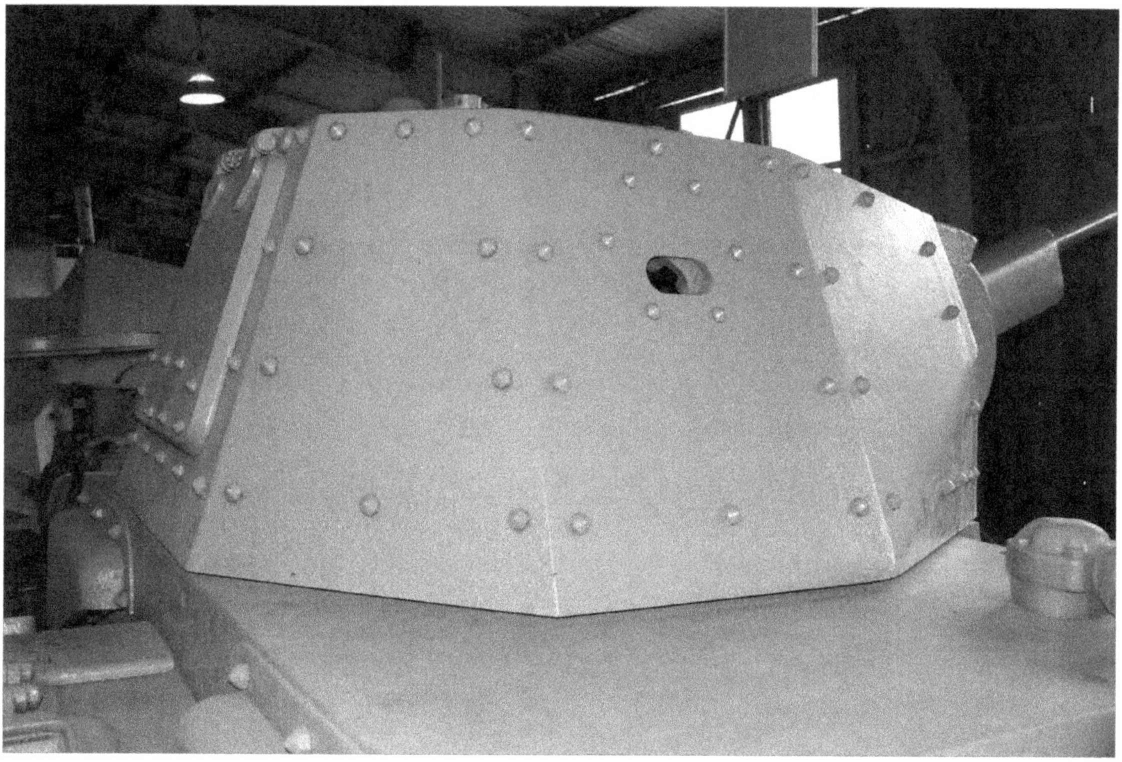

CORAZZATI ITALIANI IN RUSSIA

1941 - 1944

Semovente da 47/32 L40
XIII Gruppo Squadroni Semoventi
"Cavalleggeri di Alessandria"
1942

Carro armato leggero L3/33
III Gruppo Squadroni Corazzati
"San Giorgio" 1941

Carro armato leggero L6/40
LXVII Battaglione Bersaglieri
Motocorazzato 1942

Carro armato di preda bellica T34/76B
120° Reggimento Artiglieria 3a Divisione Celere 1942

BIBLIOGRAPHY

Books

- AA.VV., "Storia dei mezzi corazzati", Fratelli Fabbri Editori, Milano 1976.
- AA.VV., "Soldati e Battaglie della Seconda Guerra Mondiale", Hobby & Work Italiana Editrice, Bresso (MI), 1999.
- Barlozzetti Ugo, Pirella Alberto, "Mezzi dell'Esercito italiano 1935 – 1945", Editoriale Olimpia, Firenze, 1986.
- Benvenuti Bruno, Colonna Ugo, "Fronte Terra – L'armamento italiano nella Seconda Guerra Mondiale", volumi 2/I, 2/II e 2/III , Edizioni Bizzarri, Roma, 1972.
- Cappellano Filippo, Pignato Nicola, "Gli autoveicoli da combattimento dell'Esercito Italiano", volume I, S.M.E. – Ufficio Storico, Roma, 2002.
- Cappellano Filippo, Pignato Nicola, "Gli autoveicoli da combattimento dell'Esercito Italiano", volume II, S.M.E. – Ufficio Storico, Roma, 2002.
- Cappellano Filippo, Pignato Nicola, "Insegne, uniformi, distintivi e tradizioni delle Truppe Corazzate Italiane, T & T edizioni, 2005.
- Carretta Luigi, Finazzer Enrico, "Le camionette del Regio Esercito", Gruppo Modellistico Trentino, Trento, 2014.
- Carretta Luigi, Finazzer Enrico, "Le camionette del Regio Esercito", Gruppo Modellistico Trentino, Trento, 2020 (seconda edizione).
- Ceva Lucio, Curami Andrea, "La meccanizzazione dell'Esercito fino al 1943", S.M.E – Ufficio Storico, Roma, 1989.
- Crippa Paolo, "I Reparti Corazzati della Repubblica Sociale Italiana 1943 -1945", Marvia Edizioni, Voghera (PV), 2006.
- Crippa Paolo, "I mezzi corazzati italiani della guerra civile 1943-1945", Mattioli 1885, Fidenza (PR), 2015.
- Crippa Paolo, "Storia dei Reparti Corazzati della Repubblica Sociale Italiana 1943 -1945", Marvia Edizioni, Voghera (PV), 2022.
- Cucut Carlo, "Le Forze Armate della R.S.I. 1943 – 1945 – Forze di terra", G.M.T., Trento, 2005.
- Falessi Cesare, Pafi Benedetto, "Veicoli da Combattimento dell'Esercito italiano dal 1939 al 1945", Interama Books, 1976.
- Guglielmi Daniele, Tallillo Andrea, Tallillo Antonio, "Carro L3. Carri veloci, carri leggeri, derivati", GMT, Trento, 2004.
- Guglielmi Daniele, Tallillo Andrea, Tallillo Antonio, "Carro L6 – Carri leggeri, semoventi, derivati", GMT, Trento, 2007.
- Guglielmi Daniele, Tallillo Andrea, Tallillo Antonio, "Carro L6 – Carri leggeri, semoventi, derivati", GMT, Trento, 2019 (seconda edizione).
- Jowett Philip, "The Italian Army 1940 – 45 (3)", serie "Men-at-Arms", Osprey Military, UK, 2001.
- Parri Maurizio, Bianchi Carlo, "A nessuno secondi – Le ricompense al valor militare ai Carristi d'Italia dal 1927 ad oggi", Associazione nazionale Carristi d'Italia, Roma, 2021.

- Pignato Nicola, "Dalla Libia al Libano 1921/1985", Editrice Scorpione, Taranto, 1989.
- Pignato Nicola, "Automezzi da combattimento dell'Esercito Italiano 1912/1990", GMT, Trento, 1991.
- Pignato Nicola, "Motori!!! Le truppe corazzate italiane 1919 – 1994", GMT, Trento, 1995.
- Pignato Nicola, Cappellano Filippo, "Dal TL37 all'AS43", GMT, Trento, 1997.
- Pisanò Giorgio, "Gli ultimi in grigioverde", Edizioni F.P.E., Milano, 1967.
- Solari Attilio, "Dalla Russia noi siamo tornati".

Articles

- Guglielmi Daniele, Cioci Antonio, "I volontari italiani nella 2.Fallschirmjagër Division", in "Storia e& Battaglie".
- Burini Daniele, Crippa Paolo, "I Camionettisti del Gruppo Paris", in " Ritterkreuz" numero 34, anno 6, luglio 2014.
- Crippa Paolo, "Corazzati italiani in Russia 1941 – 1943", in "Fronti di guerra - Ritterkreuz" numero 78, anno 13, novembre 2021.
- Tallillo Antonio, Crippa Paolo, "Carri leggeri italiani in Russia 1941 – 1942" in "Il Carrista d'Italia", n°310 gennaio/febbraio/marzo 2022.
- Tallillo Antonio e Andrea, "Il carro L6 ed il LXVII Bersaglieri corazzato in Russia", in "Fronti di guerra - Ritterkreuz" numero 81, anno 14, maggio 2022.

Other publications

- "Memorie di un Giovane Fascista", memorie inedite di Emilio Pagani, raccolte da Daniele Burini.
- Falca Silvia, Depetroni Mauro, Plini Paolo, "Breve storia dei quattordici mesi di vita della Divisione di Fanteria Vicenza (156) – (10 marzo 1942 – 15 maggio 1943)".

Documents

- "Smobilitazione e scioglimento della Divisione di Fanteria "Vicenza" (256)", 2 maggio 1943, Archivio Storico dell'Arma dei Carabinieri.
- Testimonianza del geniere trasmettitore Eugène Lanteri-Minet, inquadrato negli equipaggi delle AB41 del "Nizza Cavalleria", riportata nel sito internet www.divisionevicenza.it.
- Pignato Nicola, D'Inzeo Fabio, "Le autoblinde AB 40, 41 e 43", articolo tratto dal sito internet www.modellismopiu.it.

SOLDIERSHOP
PUBLISHING
BOOKS TO COLLECT